NorthStar

Focus on Listening and Speaking

Basic

Laurie Frazier
Robin Mills

SERIES EDITORS
Frances Boyd
Carol Numrich

Longman

NorthStar: Focus on Listening and Speaking, Basic

Pearson Education, 10 Bank Street, White Plains, NY 10606

Editorial director: Allen Ascher
Acquisitions editor: Louisa Hellegers
Director of design and production: Rhea Banker
Development editor: Debbie Sistino
Production manager: Marie McNamara
Managing editor: Linda Moser
Production editor: Alice Vigliani
Senior manufacturing manager: Patrice Fraccio
Photo research: Diana Nott
Cover design: Rhea Banker
Text design: Delgado Design, Inc.
Cover illustration: Wassily Kandinsky's *Im Blau* © 1998 Artist Rights
    Society (ARS), New York/ADAGP, Paris
    Transparency from Kunstammlung Nordrhein-Westfalen,
    Düsseldorf, owner of the painting.
    Photograph taken by Walter Klein, Düsseldorf.
Text composition: Preface, Inc.
Text art: Lloyd Birmingham, Dusan Petricic
Photo credits: p. 7, Eric Luse/San Francisco Chronicle; p. 7, © The
    Stock Market/Chuck Savage, 1996; p. 68, © Tom Sanders/Adventure
    Photo & Film; p. 111, © Thomas Utsi; p. 114, Picture 1, ©
    Minnesota Office of Tourism; Picture 2, © Minnesota Office of
    Tourism; Picture 3, © Minnesota Office of Tourism; Picture 4, ©
    Comma Pictures, Finland; Picture 5, © Minnesota Office of
    Tourism; Picture 6, © Minnesota Office of Tourism.

Library of Congress Cataloging-in-Publication Data
Frazier, Laurie Leach.
    NorthStar. Focus on listening and speaking, basic/Laurie Frazier,
Robin Mills.
        p.   cm.
    ISBN 0-201-57179-X (pbk.)
    1. English Language—Textbooks for foreign speakers. 2. English
Language—Spoken English—Problems, exercises, etc. 3. Listening—
Problems, exercises, etc. I. Mills, Robin. II. Title.
PE1128.F6749 1998
428.3'4—dc21   97-39163
                                                          CIP

8 9 10—RNV—03

CONTENTS

INTRODUCTION

NorthStar is an innovative four-level, integrated skills series for learners of English as a Second or Foreign Language. The series is divided into two strands: listening/speaking and reading/writing. There are four books in each strand, taking students from the Basic to the Advanced level. The two books at each level explore different aspects of the same contemporary themes, which allows for reinforcement of both vocabulary and grammatical structures. Each strand and each book can also function independently as a skills course built on high-interest thematic content.

NorthStar is designed to work alongside Addison Wesley Longman's *Focus on Grammar* series, and students are referred directly to *Focus on Grammar* for further practice and detailed grammatical explanations.

NorthStar is written for students with academic as well as personal language goals, for those who want to learn English while exploring enjoyable, intellectually challenging themes.

NORTHSTAR'S PURPOSE

The *NorthStar* series grows out of our experience as teachers and curriculum designers, current research in second-language acquisition and pedagogy, as well as our beliefs about language teaching. It is based on five principles.

Principle One: In language learning, making meaning is all-important. The more profoundly students are stimulated intellectually and emotionally by what goes on in class, the more language they will use and retain. One way that classroom teachers can engage students in making meaning is by organizing language study thematically.

We have tried to identify themes that are up-to-date, sophisticated, and varied in tone—some lighter, some more serious—on ideas and issues of wide concern. The forty themes in *NorthStar* provide stimulating topics for the readings and the listening selections, including why people like dangerous sports, the effect of food on mood, an Olympic swimmer's fight against AIDS, experimental punishments for juvenile offenders, people's relationships with their cars, philanthropy, emotional intelligence, privacy in the workplace, and the influence of arts education on brain development.

Each corresponding unit of the integrated skills books explores two distinct topics related to a single theme as the chart below illustrates.

Theme	Listening/Speaking Topic	Reading/Writing Topic
Insects	Offbeat professor fails at breeding pests, then reflects on experience	Extract adapted from Kafka's "The Metamorphosis"
Personality	Shyness, a personal and cultural view	Definition of, criteria for, success

Principle Two: Second-language learners, particularly adults, need and want to learn both the form and content of the language. To accomplish this, it is useful to integrate language skills with the study of grammar, vocabulary, and American culture.

In *NorthStar,* we have integrated the skills in two strands: listening/speaking and reading/writing. Further, each thematic unit integrates the study of a grammatical point with related vocabulary and cultural information. When skills are integrated, language use inside of the classroom more closely mimics language use outside of the classroom. This motivates students. At the same time, the focus can shift back and forth from what is said to how it is said to the relationship between the two. Students are apt to use more of their senses, more of themselves. What goes on in the classroom can also appeal to a greater variety of learning styles. Gradually, the integrated-skills approach narrows the gap between the ideas and feelings students want to express in speaking and writing and their present level of English proficiency.

The link between the listening/speaking and reading/writing strands is close enough to allow students to explore the themes and review grammar and reinforce vocabulary, yet it is distinct enough to sustain their interest. Also, language levels and grammar points in *NorthStar* are keyed to Addison Wesley Longman's *Focus on Grammar* series.

Principle Three: Both teachers and students need to be active learners. Teachers must encourage students to go beyond whatever level they have reached.

With this principle in mind, we have tried to make the exercises creative, active, and varied. Several activities call for considered opinion and critical thinking. Also, the exercises offer students many opportunities for individual reflection, pair- and small-group learning, as well as out-of-class assignments for review and

research. An answer key is printed on perforated pages in the back of each book so the teacher or students can remove it. A teacher's manual, which accompanies each book, features ideas and tips for tailoring the material to individual groups of students, planning the lessons, managing the class, and assessing students' progress.

Principle Four: Feedback is essential for language learners and teachers. If students are to become better able to express themselves in English, they need a response to both what they are expressing and how they are expressing it.

NorthStar's exercises offer multiple opportunities for oral and written feedback from fellow students and from the teacher. A number of open-ended opinion and inference exercises invite students to share and discuss their answers. In information gap, presentation, and fieldwork activities, students must present and solicit information and opinions from their peers as well as members of their communities. Throughout these activities, teachers may offer feedback on the form and content of students' language, sometimes on the spot and sometimes via audio/video recordings or notes.

Principle Five: The quality of relationships among the students and between the students and teacher is important, particularly in a language class where students are asked to express themselves on issues and ideas.

The information and activities in *NorthStar* promote genuine interaction, acceptance of differences, and authentic communication. By building skills and exploring ideas, the exercises help students participate in discussions and write essays of an increasingly more complex and sophisticated nature.

DESIGN OF THE UNITS

For clarity and ease of use, the listening/speaking and reading/writing strands follow the same unit outline given below. Each unit contains from 5 to 8 hours of classroom material. Teachers can customize the units by assigning some exercises for homework and/or skipping others. Exercises in sections 1–4 are essential for comprehension of the topic, while teachers may want to select among the activities in sections 5–7.

1. **Approaching the Topic**

   A warm-up, these activities introduce students to the general context for listening or reading and get them personally connected to the topic. Typically, students might react to a visual image, describe a personal experience, or give an opinion orally or in writing.

2. **Preparing to Listen/Preparing to Read**

   In this section, students are introduced to information and language to help them comprehend the specific tape or text they will study. They might read and react to a paragraph framing the topic, prioritize factors, or take a general-knowledge quiz and share information. In the vocabulary section, students work with words and expressions selected to help them with comprehension.

3. **Listening One/Reading One**

   This sequence of four exercises guides students to listen or read with understanding and enjoyment by practicing the skills of (a) prediction, (b) comprehension of main ideas, (c) comprehension of details, and (d) inference. In activities of increasing detail and complexity, students learn to grasp and interpret meaning. The sequence culminates in an inference exercise that gets students to listen and read between the lines.

4. **Listening Two/Reading Two**

   Here students work with a tape or text that builds on ideas from the first listening/reading. This second tape or text contrasts with the first in viewpoint, genre, and/or tone. Activities ask students to explicitly relate the two pieces, consider consequences, distinguish and express points of view. In these exercises, students can attain a deeper understanding of the topic.

5. **Reviewing Language**

   These exercises help students explore, review, and play with language from both of the selections. Using the thematic context, students focus on language: pronunciation, word forms, prefixes and suffixes, word domains, idiomatic expressions, analogies. The listening/speaking strand stresses oral exercises, while the reading/writing strand focuses on written responses.

6. **Skills for Expression**

   Here students practice related grammar points across the theme in both topics. The grammar is practiced orally in the listening/speaking strand, and in writing in the reading/writing strand. For additional practice, teachers can turn to Addison Wesley Longman's *Focus on Grammar*, to which *NorthStar* is keyed by level and grammar points. In the Style section, students practice functions (listening/speaking) or rhetorical styles (reading/writing) that prepare them to express ideas on a higher level. Within each unit, students are led from controlled to freer practice of productive skills.

7. **On Your Own**

   These activities ask students to apply the content, language, grammar, and style they have practiced in the unit. The exercises elicit a higher level of speaking or writing than students were capable of at the start of the unit. Speaking topics include role plays, surveys, presentations, and experiments. Writing topics include paragraphs, letters, summaries, and academic essays.

In Fieldwork, the second part of On Your Own, students go outside of the classroom, using their knowledge and skills to gather data from personal interviews, library research, and telephone or Internet research. They report and reflect on the data in oral or written presentations to the class.

AN INVITATION

We think of a good textbook as a musical score or a movie script: It tells you the moves and roughly how quickly and in what sequence to make them. But until you and your students bring it to life, a book is silent and static, a mere possibility. We hope that *NorthStar* orients, guides, and interests you as teachers.

It is our hope that the *NorthStar* series stimulates your students' thinking, which in turn stimulates their language learning, and that they will have many opportunities to reflect on the viewpoints of journalists, commentators, researchers, other students, and people in the community. Further, we hope that *NorthStar* guides them to develop their own viewpoint on the many and varied themes encompassed by this series.

We welcome your comments and questions. Please send them to us at the publisher:

Frances Boyd and Carol Numrich, Editors
NorthStar
Addison Wesley Longman
10 Bank Street
White Plains, NY 10606-1951
or, by e-mail at:
awlelt@awl.com

ACKNOWLEDGMENTS

We would like to thank Raymond Tucci and Johannes Frazier for their patience and support throughout this project. Thanks to Johannes also for his help with the photography.

Laurie Frazier
Robin Mills

OFFBEAT JOBS

Doctor
$105,000

Professional
Basketball
Player
$1,500,000

Salesclerk
$14,000

Chef
$23,000

Architect
$40,000

Police Officer
$38,000

1 APPROACHING THE TOPIC

A. PREDICTING

Look at the pictures of the people. Read the title of the unit.
Discuss these questions with the class.

1. Which job has the highest salary? Which job has the lowest salary? Why?

2. Should any of the jobs have a higher or lower salary? Why?

3. What do you think the title of the unit means?

B. SHARING INFORMATION

1 *Look at the list of things to consider when choosing a job. Rank the items in order of importance from 1 to 7. Number 1 is the most important and number 7 is the least important.*

_____ salary (how much money you make)

_____ hours (what hours you work)

_____ safety (how safe the work is)

_____ workplace (indoors, outdoors, in an office)

_____ interest (how much you like the work)

_____ demand (how easy it is to find a job)

_____ education (how much schooling you need for the job)

2 *Now compare your answers in a group. Tell why each item is important or not important to you.*

Example:

A: I think salary is important because I need to make money for my family.

B: I think interest is important because I want a job that I like.

PREPARING TO LISTEN

A. BACKGROUND

There are good and bad points about every job. So when choosing the best job for yourself, you need to think carefully about what is most important to you. It's also a good idea to think about your skills and interests. Skills are abilities, or things you do well, and interests are things you like to do. Most people are happy with a job that matches their skills and their interests.

Look at the words to describe jobs and people. Then look at the jobs in the chart. Choose two words to describe each job. Then choose at least one skill and one interest that you think is important for a person who does each job. Use the words below and think of your own. Then compare your answers with a partner.

JOBS

What's the job like?

interesting or boring

tiring or relaxing

safe or dangerous

high-paying or low-paying

difficult or easy

_____

_____

_____

_____

_____

_____

PEOPLE

What skills are important?

artistic

careful

creative

educated

friendly

good with your hands

hardworking

strong / athletic

_____

_____

_____

What interests are important?

Like to work:

  alone

  with people

  with food

  with money

  indoors

  outdoors

_____

_____

_____

JOB	WHAT'S THE JOB LIKE?	WHAT SKILLS ARE IMPORTANT?	WHAT INTERESTS ARE IMPORTANT?
chef			
salesclerk			
police officer			
architect			
doctor			
professional basketball player			

B. VOCABULARY FOR COMPREHENSION

Read the sentences. Then choose the best words to complete the definitions of the underlined words.

1. I work in a computer <u>factory</u>. I help make computers.
   A <u>factory</u> is a _____.

   a. building where things are made   **b.** job making things

2. I like to <u>taste</u> food while I'm cooking to make sure it is good.
   To <u>taste</u> something means to _____.

   a. eat all of something   **b.** try food by eating a little bit

3. Chefs are <u>creative</u>. They think of new ways to cook food.
   To be <u>creative</u> is to _____.

   a. make food   **b.** think of new things

4. I'm a dog walker. I really like my job, but people are often surprised
   when I tell them my job because it's so <u>offbeat</u>.
   Something that is <u>offbeat</u> is something _____.

   a. different or unusual   **b.** you like

5. I love ice cream because it has a sweet <u>flavor</u>.
   A <u>flavor</u> is something that _____.

   a. has its own special taste   **b.** is good to eat

6. I love to eat <u>spicy</u> food such as Thai food and Mexican food.
   <u>Spicy</u> food is food that _____.

   a. is from a different country   **b.** has a strong flavor from spices

7. My friend was a <u>contestant</u> on a game show once. She answered
   some of the questions right and won $2,000.
   A <u>contestant</u> is someone who _____.

   a. wins money   **b.** plays a game

8. I like to listen to a radio talk show every morning. The <u>host</u> is
   interesting, and she's funny, too.
   A <u>host</u> is someone who _____.

   a. talks to guests on a radio   **b.** is interesting
      or TV program

9. I have an <u>insurance policy</u> for my car. If I have an accident and my car is damaged, the insurance company will pay me some money. An <u>insurance policy</u> is _____.

    a. an agreement with an insurance company to be paid money in case of an accident, illness, or death

    b. money you are paid when you have an accident

10. I have sensitive <u>taste buds</u>. I don't like to eat spicy foods because they burn my mouth.
<u>Taste buds</u> are _____.

    a. spicy foods   **b.** the parts of the tongue that can taste food

3 LISTENING ONE: What's My Job?

A. INTRODUCING THE TOPIC

Listen to the beginning of What's My Job? *Then answer the questions.*

1. You are listening to a _____.

    a. job interview   **b.** game show   **c.** radio show

2. Wayne is a _____.

    a. host   **b.** contestant   **c.** guest

3. Rita is a _____.

    a. host   **b.** contestant   **c.** guest

4. Peter is going to describe _____.

    a. his job   **b.** his company   **c.** himself

5. What do you think Peter will talk about? Circle more than one answer.

    a. what he does   **b.** where he works   **c.** how much money he makes

    d. his skills   **e.** his interests

B. LISTENING FOR MAIN IDEAS

You will listen to a game show about offbeat jobs. Peter will talk about his job. Read the statements. Circle the best answer to complete each sentence.

1. Rita asks Peter _____ questions.
   a. two   **b.** three   **c.** four

2. Peter works in a _____.
   a. restaurant   **b.** factory   **c.** bakery

3. Peter is _____.
   a. a factory worker   **b.** a chef   **c.** an ice-cream taster

4. Peter has to be careful with _____.
   a. his taste buds   **b.** the ice cream   **c.** the factory machines

5. The people in Peter's family have been _____ for a long time.
   a. ice-cream tasters   **b.** in the restaurant business   **c.** in the ice-cream business

C. LISTENING FOR DETAILS

Listen again. Read the sentences. Decide if they are true or false. Write T or F on the lines.

_____ 1. Peter can be creative at work.

_____ 2. Peter thinks of new ice-cream flavors.

_____ 3. He eats all the ice cream at work.

_____ 4. He doesn't eat spicy foods.

_____ 5. He doesn't drink alcohol or coffee.

_____ 6. He smokes.

_____ 7. He has a one million–dollar insurance policy for his taste buds.

_____ 8. He studied ice-cream tasting in school.

Now go back to Section 3A on page 5. Were your predictions correct?

D. LISTENING BETWEEN THE LINES

Listen to the excerpts from Listening One. Discuss your answers to the questions with the class.

Excerpt One

1. Does Wayne say that Peter's job is easy or difficult?

2. Listen to Wayne's tone of voice. What do you think Wayne really thinks about Peter's job?

3. Do you think Peter's job is difficult or easy? Why do you think so?

4. Do you think you could do Peter's job?

Excerpt Two

1. Did Peter go to ice-cream tasting school?

2. Listen to Wayne's tone of voice. Why do you think he asks Peter that question?

3. How did Peter get started as an ice-cream taster?

4. What do you think is the best way to get started in a job?

4 LISTENING TWO: More Offbeat Jobs

A. EXPANDING THE TOPIC

❶ *Look at the pictures above. Where does each person work? What job is each person doing?*

② *Listen to the people talking about their jobs. Write the number of the conversation under the correct picture on page 7.*

③ *Listen again. Look at the statements in the chart. Write* **WW** *if the statement is true for the window washer and* **PS** *if the statement is true for the professional shopper. Some statements may be true for both. The first one is done for you.*

a. I like my job.	WW, PS
b. I work outdoors.	
c. I earn a high salary.	
d. My work is dangerous.	
e. I like to work with people.	
f. I'm good with money.	
g. I'm good with my hands.	
h. My work is tiring.	
i. It was difficult to get started in this job.	
j. I have my own business.	

B. LINKING LISTENINGS ONE AND TWO

① *You have learned about some unusual jobs. Read the following questions and write* **1, 2,** *or* **3** *for each one.*

1 = ice-cream taster

2 = window washer

3 = professional shopper

Then compare your answers in a group. Explain your answers.

Example: I think the ice-cream taster's job is the most unusual because I don't think there are very many ice-cream tasters.

Which job do you think is . . .

_____ the most unusual?   _____ the most difficult?

_____ the most tiring?   _____ the most important?

_____ the most relaxing?   _____ the most dangerous?

_____ the most offbeat?   _____ the highest paid?

2 *Which job would you most like to have? Which job wouldn't you like to have? Explain.*

5 REVIEWING LANGUAGE

A. EXPLORING LANGUAGE: Syllable Stress

In words with more than one syllable, one syllable is stressed. Stressed syllables sound longer than unstressed syllables. They are also louder and higher in pitch than unstressed syllables.

Listen to these examples:

ca<u>re</u>ful

pro<u>fes</u>sional

hard<u>work</u>ing

1 *Listen to the words. Write the number of syllables you hear in each word. Then listen again and underline the stressed syllable.*

_____ **1.** friendly

_____ **2.** important

_____ **3.** relaxing

_____ **4.** educated

_____ **5.** creative

② *Work with another student. Student A, say each word in your list. Be sure to lengthen the stressed syllable. Student B, look at Student Activities, page 159. Listen to Student A say each word, and underline the syllable that is stressed. Then change roles. Check your answers.*

Student A	**Student A**
Say:	*Listen and underline:*
1. <u>sales</u>clerk	6. restaurant
2. <u>diff</u>icult	7. insurance
3. po<u>lice</u>	8. taste buds
4. out<u>doors</u>	9. spicy
5. un<u>u</u>sual	10. athletic

B. WORKING WITH WORDS

① *Work in pairs. One student reads A's line. The other student completes the sentence in B's line with a word or phrase from the list on the left. Both sentences should have the same meaning. Use the underlined words to help you. Switch roles after item 3. Check the answers in the Answer Key.*

be careful

get started

interesting

lucky

quit

salary

1. A: I don't like my job. I want to <u>leave</u> it.

   B: You want to _____ your job.

2. A: I like my job. It is <u>never boring</u>.

   B: Your job is _____.

3. A: A cashier must count money <u>carefully.</u>

   B: A cashier needs to _____ _____ with money.

4. A: It's difficult to <u>begin</u> working as a doctor.

   B: It's difficult to _____ _____ as a doctor.

5. A: A professional basketball player makes a lot of <u>money</u>.

   B: A basketball player has a high _____.

6. A: I was walking down the street and <u>by chance</u> I found fifty dollars on the sidewalk.

   B: You were _____ to find the money.

2 *Work in pairs. Read the conversation. Fill in the blanks with the correct words from Exercise 1 on page 10. Then practice reading the conversation out loud with your partner.*

A: So what do you do?

B: I'm a dog walker.

A: A dog walker? That's an unusual job!

B: Yes, it is offbeat, but it's never boring. It's an

(1) _____ job.

A: So how did you (2) _____ _____ as a

dog walker?

B: Well, I used to walk my dog in the park every day. I met some

people there with dogs. They didn't have time to walk their dogs,

so I started to walk their dogs for them.

A: Do you have another job?

B: No, I was an accountant. But I got tired of working in an office,

so I (3) _____ my job to become a full-time dog

walker. Now I only walk dogs. The only problem is that I don't

make as much money. The (4) _____ isn't as good

as my old job.

A: Really? Is there anything else you don't like about your job?

B: Well, it is difficult to take care of a lot of dogs at the same time.

They can run fast. I have to (5) _____

_____ not to lose a dog. But even so, I really love

my job.

A: That's nice. You're (6) _____ to have a job you

enjoy. Keep up the good work!

6 SKILLS FOR EXPRESSION

A. GRAMMAR: Descriptive Adjectives

❶ *Read the questions and answers. Look at the words in italics. Then answer the questions below.*

- ◆ What's your job like?   My job is *interesting*.

- ◆ What kind of person are you?   I'm a *friendly* person.

a. Look at the answers to the questions. What is the verb in each sentence?

b. What is the noun in each sentence?

c. Which words describe the nouns? Where do they come in the sentences?

Descriptive Adjectives

FOCUS ON GRAMMAR

See Descriptive Adjectives in *Focus on Grammar, Basic.*

Adjectives describe nouns.

a. Adjectives can come after the verb **be.**
   - ◆ My job **is tiring.**

b. Adjectives can also come before a noun.
   - ◆ Architects are **creative people.**

c. When a singular noun follows an adjective, use **a** before the adjective if the adjective begins with a consonant sound.
   - ◆ Teaching isn't **a high-paying job.**

d. When a singular noun follows an adjective, use **an** before the adjective if the adjective begins with a vowel sound.
   - ◆ Ice-cream tasting is **an unusual job.**

❷ *Work with another student. Take turns making sentences using the nouns and adjectives in the list on page 13. After you say each sentence, tell if you think the sentence is true or not true. Say "that's true" or "that's not true." If you don't think the sentence is true, change it to make it true.*

Example: A: A secretary's work is dangerous.

B: That's not true. A secretary's work isn't dangerous. It's safe.

1. a secretary's work / dangerous

2. doctors / educated

3. a teacher's job / difficult

4. police officers / hardworking people

5. window washing / interesting job

6. professional basketball players / important

7. cooking / relaxing job

❸ *Work in a small group. One person thinks of a job and makes three sentences about the job. Look at Section 2A on pages 2–3 for a list of adjectives, or think of your own. The other students ask yes/no questions to guess the job. Then change roles until everyone in your group describes a job.*

Example: A: I am creative. My job is unusual. My job is important.

B: Are you an architect?

A: No, I'm not.

C: Are you an ice-cream taster?

B. STYLE: Small Talk

When making conversation, it's polite to ask about a person's job and interests. It's also polite to express interest when people tell you something about themselves.

Asking about someone's job and interests	Talking about yourself	Showing interest
What do you do?	I'm not working right now.	Oh . . .
	I'm a . . . (student, chef, homemaker).	Really?
	I'm retired.	That's interesting.
What do you like to do in your free time?	I like to . . . (listen to music).	That's nice.
What do you enjoy doing?	I enjoy . . . (working outdoors).	

❶ *Work with another student. Complete the conversation with your own information. Then practice it out loud.*

A: Hi. My name's _____.

B: Hi. I'm _____. Nice to meet you.

A: Nice to meet you, too. So what do you do?

B: I'm _____.

A: _____.

B: How about you? What do you do?

A: _____.

B: _____. So what do you like to do in your free time?

A: _____. How about you?

B: _____.

❷ *Walk around the classroom and talk to six other students. Write each person's name, job, and one interest on a separate piece of paper. Then introduce the students to the class.*

Example: This is Mark. He's a student. He likes to cook.

This is Eva. She's a homemaker. She enjoys dancing.

7 ON YOUR OWN

A. SPEAKING TOPICS: A Skills and Interests Interview

❶ *You have listened to some other people talk about their skills and interests. Now, think about your own skills and interests. Fill out the following chart about yourself. Check yes or no for each question. If you answer yes, explain or give an example. Then work with another student. Ask the questions and write your partner's answers.*

Example: A: Are you artistic?

B: Yes, I am. I can paint.

A: Oh, really? That's interesting!

	YOU			YOUR PARTNER		
Skills						
Are you . . .	**Yes**	**No**	**Explain**	**Yes**	**No**	**Explain**
artistic?						
creative?						
strong or athletic?						
careful?						
hardworking?						
friendly?						
educated?						
good with computers?						
good with your hands?						
good with language(s)?						
Interests						
Do you like						
to work . . .	**Yes**	**No**	**Explain**	**Yes**	**No**	**Explain**
alone?						
with people?						
with food?						
with money?						
outdoors?						
at home?						
in an office?						

2 *Now choose a job that you think is good for your partner. Think of a job from the unit or a different one.*

❸ *Introduce your partner to the class. Tell the class which job you think is good for your partner and use the information in the chart to tell why.*

Listening Task

As you listen to your classmates, write down the names of three students who have the same skills or interests that you do. Do you agree with the jobs their partners recommend?

Students	**Skill or Interest**
1. _____	_____
2. _____	_____
3. _____	_____

B. FIELDWORK

Think of an offbeat job or a job you would like to have. Go to the library or look on the Internet to get information about the job. Report back to the class about it. In your report, include the information below.

Job Title: _____

Workplace: _____

Skills and Interests for the Job: _____

Why the Job Is Interesting: _____

Listening Task

Listen to your classmates' reports. Which job do you think is most interesting? Why?

A PIECE OF THE COUNTRY IN THE CITY

1 APPROACHING THE TOPIC

A. PREDICTING

Look at the picture. Read the title of the unit. Discuss these questions with the class.

1. Which parts of the picture are the city, the suburbs, and the country? Point to them. How do you know?

2. What do you think the title of the unit means?

B. SHARING INFORMATION

Work in groups and discuss these questions. Use the words on the left to help you.

apartments
crowded
dangerous
farms
gardens
highways
houses
malls
nature
neighborhoods
quiet
safe
stores
traffic
trees

1. How is the city different from the suburbs? How is it different from the country?

   The city is _____.

   The country is _____.

   The suburbs are _____.

   The city has _____.

   The country has _____.

   The suburbs have _____.

2. Which part of the picture on page 17 is like the place where you live now? Why?

3. Which place do you prefer? Why?

2 PREPARING TO LISTEN

A. BACKGROUND

Read the paragraph. Then follow the directions below.

In 1900, 60 percent of the people in the United States lived in the country and 40 percent lived in the city. By 1990, 75 percent of the population was urban, or lived in the city, and only 25 percent was rural, or lived in the country. With more and more people living in cities, cities are getting bigger. Now, more cities are starting programs called "urban greening." Urban greening programs create more green areas in cities. Urban greening programs make places for people to enjoy nature. Parks and gardens are examples of urban greening programs. Urban greening is a way to have a little piece of the country in the city.

Work in a group. Write the names of the other students in your group in the chart on page 19. Then write each student's answers to the questions in the chart. When you are finished, have one student tell the class about your group's answers.

Example: "One student has a garden, and three students don't have gardens."

NAMES			
1. Do you (or someone you know) have a garden?			
2. Can you have a garden where you live? Why or why not?			
3. Why do you think people have gardens?			
4. What do you think *community gardens* are?			

B. VOCABULARY FOR COMPREHENSION

Read the sentences. Choose the best definition of the underlined words from the list on page 20. Write the correct letter of the definition in the blanks.

1. I saw a beautiful <u>community garden</u> today. Many people worked together and made one large garden.

2. People can <u>grow</u> many things in a garden. Some people grow vegetables and other food. Other people grow flowers.

3. There are many apartment buildings and houses on my street, but one area doesn't have any buildings on it. It's an <u>empty lot</u>. There's nothing there.

4. Many people in my neighborhood enjoy their gardens. They put many things in their gardens. They <u>plant</u> vegetables and flowers.

5. Sometimes people throw paper, soda cans, and other <u>garbage</u> on the ground. It's better to put it in a garbage can.

6. I live in a small house, but there is a nice big <u>yard</u> behind my house. I enjoy sitting outside in my yard.

7. There is an old tree in front of my house. I will take the tree away. I will <u>remove</u> it.

8. Some people use <u>drugs</u>. Some drugs, like medicines, are good. Other drugs can be dangerous.

9. I enjoy trees, flowers, and the mountains. I really like <u>nature</u>.

10. On the weekends, my family likes to go to <u>the country</u>. We drive for a few hours far away from the city so we can enjoy the trees and plants.

_____ 1. community garden

_____ 2. grow

_____ 3. empty lot

_____ 4. plant

_____ 5. garbage

_____ 6. yard

_____ 7. remove

_____ 8. drugs

_____ 9. nature

_____ 10. the country

a. take away

b. to have flowers or vegetables in a garden

c. trees, flowers, mountains, and other things outside

d. paper and other things people don't want anymore

e. an area of land next to or behind a house

f. a place far from the city where people go to enjoy nature

g. something like medicines but can be dangerous, like cocaine

h. to put seeds in the ground to become flowers or vegetables

i. a garden that many people make together

j. an area of land with no buildings on it

3 LISTENING ONE: Community Gardens

A. INTRODUCING THE TOPIC

Listen to Laura Lee talking about community gardens. Then answer the questions.

1. What are you listening to?

   a. a TV news show
   b. a radio news show
   c. a phone conversation

2. Where is the woman?

   a. in the radio studio
   b. in her yard
   c. at a community garden

3. What do you think she will learn about community gardens?
   Check (✔) more than one.

   _____ what the people plant

   _____ what people do in community gardens

   _____ how many community gardens are in New York

   _____ why the garden is important

B. LISTENING FOR MAIN IDEAS

There are many reasons to have a community garden. Here is a list of several reasons. Listen to the complete radio interview. Check (✔) the reasons the man tells the reporter.

_____ **1.** Community gardens make neighborhoods look nice.

_____ **2.** Community gardens are good places for people to enjoy nature.

_____ **3.** Community gardens are good places to walk dogs.

_____ **4.** Community gardens are good places to grow food.

_____ **5.** Community gardens are good places to grow flowers to sell.

C. LISTENING FOR DETAILS

Listen again. Check (✓) the statements that are true.

_____ 1. Ten years ago this was an empty lot.

_____ 2. One person in the neighborhood planted the community garden.

_____ 3. Before the garden, there was garbage on the empty lot.

_____ 4. There are enough apartment buildings in New York.

_____ 5. The neighbors made the neighborhood a nice place to live.

_____ 6. Before the garden, there wasn't a place to sit and relax.

_____ 7. Now, people sell vegetables, not drugs.

_____ 8. The man grew up in the country.

_____ 9. The man has a yard at his apartment.

_____ 10. Tomorrow night the radio show will be about the city's plans.

Now go back to Section 3A on page 21. Were your predictions correct?

D. LISTENING BETWEEN THE LINES

Listen to the excerpts from Listening One. Then answer the questions with a partner.

Excerpt One

1. What does the city want to do?

2. How does the man feel about the city's plans? Why?

3. What do you think the city should do? Why?

Excerpt Two

1. Why can't people in the city grow food?

2. Why do you think the man likes to grow food?

3. Do you like to work in a garden and grow food? Why or why not?

LISTENING TWO: Let's Hear from Our Listeners

A. EXPANDING THE TOPIC

Work with a partner. Look at the pictures. Then read the questions in the chart and write your answers in the "Before You Listen" column. Then, listen to the radio call-in show about urban greening and city beautification. Answer the questions. Write the answers in the "After You Listen" column.

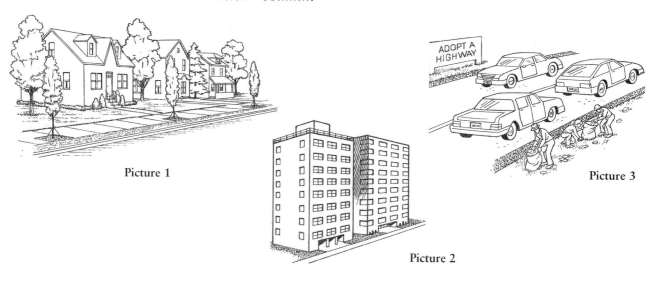

Picture 1

Picture 2

Picture 3

	BEFORE YOU LISTEN	AFTER YOU LISTEN
1. Who do you think planted the trees in picture 1?		
2. Do you think there is a garden in picture 2? Where?		
3. What are the people doing in picture 3? Why?		

B. LINKING LISTENINGS ONE AND TWO

Discuss these questions with the class.

1. Do most people in your country live in the city, the suburbs, or the country? Explain.

2. Does the place you come from have urban greening programs such as parks or gardens? How do people use them?

3. Do you think urban greening is important? Why or why not?

5 REVIEWING LANGUAGE

A. EXPLORING LANGUAGE

The regular past tense is written by adding *-ed* to a verb. For example, *walk* becomes *walked*. The regular past tense has three pronunciations: /t/, /d/ and /ɪd/. The pronunciation depends on the last sound in the base verb.

RULES

1. The final *-ed* is pronounced /ɪd/ after /t/ and /d/. /ɪd/ adds a syllable to the verb.

2. The final *-ed* is pronounced /t/ after the sounds /f/, /k/, /p/, /s/, /ʃ/, and /tʃ/.

3. The final *-ed* is pronounced /d/ after vowels.

4. The final *-ed* is pronounced /d/ after all other sounds.

❶ *Pronounce these verbs. Which rule helps you choose the correct pronunciation? Write the number of the rule next to the verbs.*

base form	regular past tense
_____ want	wanted
_____ travel	traveled
_____ play	played
_____ look	looked

❷ *Underline the verb in each sentence. Then listen to these sentences and write the verb under the correct sound in the chart. Finally, read the sentences aloud. The first one has been done for you.*

1. I <u>worked</u> in a community garden yesterday.

2. She planted some vegetables last week.

3. My children played on an empty lot near my home.

4. I walked on a beautiful tree-lined street today.

5. Last week, the city removed the garbage from the empty lot.

6. Everyone liked the flowers in the community garden.

7. My family lived in a city last year.

8. They stayed in the garden late yesterday.

9. I wanted to visit the country last weekend.

10. We watched the children playing.

/t/	/ɪd/	/d/
worked		

❸ *Think of two more verbs for the different pronunciations of the past tense ending. Write them under the correct sound.*

B. WORKING WITH WORDS

❶ *Match the words on the left with the definitions on the right.*

_____ 1. community garden
_____ 2. empty lot
_____ 3. get together
_____ 4. grow up
_____ 5. hang around
_____ 6. roof garden
_____ 7. urban greening
_____ 8. relax

a. putting green areas in a city; parks and gardens

b. not work, have free time to rest

c. a garden on top of a building

d. a garden many people grow together

e. stay in one place not doing anything

f. an area with no buildings on it

g. become an adult; get older

h. meet with people

❷ *Work in pairs. Read the conversation. Fill in the blanks with the correct words from Exercise 1. Use the underlined words to help you. Then practice the conversation with your partner.*

A: Good afternoon. This is Radio Call In on WNYZ. How can I help you today?

B: Well, my neighborhood really needs something to <u>make it more beautiful and green</u>.

A: Hmm. So you are looking for ideas about (**1**) _____ _____?

B: Yes. Do you have any?

A: Well, there are many things you can do. First of all, you should try to <u>meet with all your neighbors</u>.

B: OK. I'll try to (**2**) _____ _____ with everyone.

A: Then you can discuss ideas. For example, you can plant <u>gardens on top of the apartment buildings</u>.

B: OK, maybe a (**3**) _____ _____. That's a good idea.

A: Yes, and people can go there after work to just <u>sit and rest</u>.

B: Yes, that would be a nice place to (**4**) _____.

A: Or if there is <u>an area with no buildings on it</u>, you could plant a community garden.

B: Yes, we have an (5) _____ _____. And now, a lot of <u>people stand there doing nothing</u>.

A: Yes, people will (6) _____ _____ empty lots.

B: These are good ideas. Thanks. You know, when I was a child, I lived in the country and we had a lot of green areas. Then, when I <u>became an adult</u>, I moved to the city. Things sure are different here!

A: Yes, things change when we (7) _____ _____. Well, I hope you use some urban greening ideas in your neighborhood.

B: OK, I will. Thanks. Bye-bye.

SKILLS FOR EXPRESSION

A. GRAMMAR: Simple Past Tense

❶ *Read the sentences. Then answer the questions below.*

- ◆ I lived in the suburbs three years ago.
- ◆ She didn't plant flowers last week.
- ◆ Last year, they grew vegetables.

a. Do the sentences talk about the past, the present, or the future? How do you know?

b. Underline the verbs. Which verbs are regular? Which are irregular? How do you know?

Simple Past Tense

FOCUS ON GRAMMAR

See Simple Past Tense in
Focus on Grammar, Basic.

a. Use the simple past tense to talk about an event in the past.

  ◆ Ten years ago, before we **planted** this garden, it was just an empty lot.

b. To form the regular simple past tense, add **-ed** to most verbs.

  ◆ I **walked** in the park this morning.

c. To form the irregular past tense, change the form of the verb.

  ◆ We **grew** vegetables in our garden last year.

d. To form a negative statement, use **did not** or **didn't** plus the base form of the verb.

  ◆ I **didn't live** in the suburbs last year.

e. Time markers for the past tense come at the beginning or the end of the sentence.

  ◆ **Yesterday,** I walked in the country.

  ◆ I went to the city **last week.**

  Other time markers:
    yesterday morning / afternoon / evening
    the day before yesterday
    last week / month / Sunday / year / summer / night
    a week / month / year ago

f. The verb form is the same for all persons.

  ◆ **I/She/They** planted flowers last summer.

❷ *Write the past tense for these verbs. Some are regular and some are irregular. Look in a dictionary for help. Then add six more verbs you know.*

walk _____   have _____

work _____   make _____

grow _____   look _____

live _____   is _____

go _____   are _____

wear _____   arrive _____

move _____   speak _____

_____   _____

_____   _____

_____   _____

❸ *Work in pairs. Look at the time line describing important dates in Carlos's life. Student A makes a statement about Carlos. Student B says, "That's right," or "That's wrong." If the statement is wrong, Student B makes the correct statement. Then switch roles.*

Important Dates in Carlos's Life

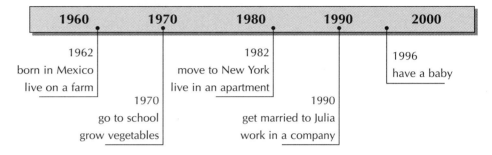

1960	1970	1980	1990	2000

1962
born in Mexico
live on a farm

1970
go to school
grow vegetables

1982
move to New York
live in an apartment

1990
get married to Julia
work in a company

1996
have a baby

Example: Student A: Carlos moved to New York in 1982.

Student B: That's right.

Student B: Carlos lived on a farm in 1990.

Student A: That's wrong. He didn't live on a farm in 1990. He lived in the city.

B. STYLE: Expressing Agreement

Agreeing in Conversation

In conversation, when we want to agree with something someone is saying, we can use the word ***too.***

• A: I like movies.

• B: I like movies, *too.*

If someone makes a negative statement that we agree with, we can use ***don't . . . either.***

• A: I don't live in the country.

• B: I *don't* live in the country *either.*

Both *too* and *don't . . . either* show agreement. *Too* is used in affirmative statements and *don't . . . either* is used with negative statements.

❶ *Work in pairs. Circle the correct response in each sentence. Then practice reading the sentences out loud.*

1. A: I work in a city.

   B: I work in a city either / too.

2. A: My family doesn't live in this city.

   B: My family doesn't live here either / too.

3. A: I lived in the suburbs when I was a child.

   B: I lived in the suburbs either / too.

4. A: I didn't have a garden three years ago.

   B: I didn't have a garden too / either.

5. A: My apartment doesn't have a yard.

   B: My apartment doesn't have a yard either / too.

6. A: I like to grow flowers.

   B: I like to grow flowers too / either.

7. A: My neighborhood doesn't have a community garden.

   B: My neighborhood doesn't have one too / either.

8. A: There's a yard behind my house.

   B: There's a yard behind my house too / either.

❷ **Part A:**

Look at the chart on page 31. Write past tense statements about yourself for each activity in the first column. They can be affirmative or negative. Then add three more activities and write past tense statements.

Part B:

*Work in groups of three. One student reads a statement from his or her chart. The other students make a statement to express agreement using **too** or **don't . . . either**. (If you don't agree, make a past tense statement about the activity.) Write the responses in the chart.*

	YOU	_____ (NAME)	_____ (NAME)
1. study English this morning	I studied English this morning.	Marta studied English this morning, too.	Henri didn't study English this morning.
2. yesterday listen to music			
3. go to a park last week			
4. last year live in a city			
5.			
6.			
7.			

ON YOUR OWN

A. SPEAKING TOPICS: Telling about a Place

Think of a place you have gone to enjoy nature. It may be your yard, a park in your city, the country, or a place you have been for vacation. Answer the questions on page 32. Then work in a small group. Tell the other students in your group about the place. You can bring a picture of the place to show other students.

PLACE: _____

1. Was the place in the city, the suburbs, or the country?

_____

2. When did you go there? Why did you go?

_____

3. What did you see there? Describe it.

_____

4. What did you do there? Describe your activities.

_____

5. How did you find out about the place? (e.g., Did a friend tell you?)

_____

6. Is there other information you want to add?

_____

B. FIELDWORK

Observe your city, town, or school campus. What urban greening programs do you see? What do people do to have a piece of the country in the city? Work with another student. Go out into your city, town, or campus and answer these questions.

1. How many yards did you see?

2. How many gardens did you see?

3. What do people grow?

4. Did you see any community gardens?

5. Did you see trees? Roof gardens?

6. What other urban greening or city beautification did you see?

Report to the class about what you saw.

A PENNY SAVED IS
A PENNY EARNED

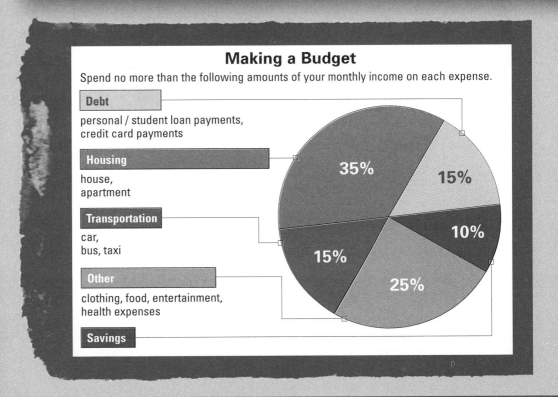

Making a Budget

Spend no more than the following amounts of your monthly income on each expense.

Debt
personal / student loan payments,
credit card payments

Housing
house,
apartment

Transportation
car,
bus, taxi

Other
clothing, food, entertainment,
health expenses

Savings

35% 15% 10% 25% 15%

1 APPROACHING THE TOPIC

A. PREDICTING

The graph above shows a monthly budget. It shows savings and expenses, how much money a person should save, and how much money a person should spend on certain things. Study the graph. Then discuss the answers to these questions with the class.

1. According to the graph, what percentage of your monthly income should you use for housing, transportation, and debt payments? What percentage of your income should you save every month? Do you agree with these amounts?

2. The title of the unit is a famous American saying. What do you think it means?

B. SHARING INFORMATION

Work in a small group. Ask three other students these questions and write their answers below. Then share the answers with the class.

	Name: _____	Name: _____	Name: _____
1. Do you have a budget?	_____	_____	_____
2. Do you think making a budget is a good idea? Why or why not?	_____	_____	_____
3. What is your biggest expense?	_____	_____	_____
4. What is your smallest expense?	_____	_____	_____

2 PREPARING TO LISTEN

A. BACKGROUND

Some people have big incomes. They earn a lot of money. Some people have small incomes. They don't earn very much money. But everyone must be careful when they spend money. If you spend more money than you earn, you owe money and you go into debt.

People must also choose the best way to pay for their expenses. One way to pay for things is with cash. Another way to pay for something is with a credit card. A credit card is a small plastic card used to buy things and pay later. A third way is to get a loan. When you take out a loan, you borrow money from a person or a bank and pay the money back later. Whenever you owe money on credit cards or loans, you have to pay interest. You have to pay extra money on the money you owe. In the United States, many people are in debt because they spend too much money using credit cards and loans.

Work in pairs. Discuss your answers to the questions. Then compare your answers with the class.

1. Which expenses do you pay for with cash? Which ones do you pay for with credit cards? Which ones do you pay for with loans?

2. Are credit cards popular in your culture? Do you like to use credit cards? Why or why not?

3. Are many people in your culture in debt? What are some reasons people go into debt?

B. VOCABULARY FOR COMPREHENSION

1 *Read the sentences. Then choose the best words to complete the definitions of the underlined words.*

1. Today I got a bill from the telephone company. It was for eighty-five dollars. I need to get the money to pay it.

   A bill is _____.

   a. a paper listing things and how much to pay for them

   b. money you pay for something

2. I don't have a very big salary. I only earn $10,000 a year.

   To earn money means to _____ money.

   a. pay

   b. get

3. I like to spend my money. I like to buy lots of things.

   To spend money means to _____ money.

   a. pay

   b. get

4. I want to save some money so I can buy a car. Every month I put $100 in the bank. In a few months I'll have enough money for the car I want.

   To save money means to _____.

   a. keep money

   b. buy something

5. I need to be more careful with my money. I need to make a budget so I'll know how much money I earn and how much I can spend every month.

   A budget is _____.

   a. how much money you get every month

   b. a plan of income and expenses for a period of time

6. Some people talk to a friend or family member for advice when they have money problems. In the United States, some people also talk to a money <u>advisor</u> who can help them with their money problems.

   An <u>advisor</u> is someone who _____.

   a. loans money   **b.** helps people with problems

7. I got a bank loan to buy my house. Every month I send a <u>payment</u> to the bank.

   A <u>payment</u> is an amount of money that _____.

   a. is paid   **b.** is saved

8. I don't like to use credit cards. I always pay for things with <u>cash</u>. <u>Cash</u> is _____.

   a. coins and paper money   **b.** credit cards

9. I live in an apartment. Every month I pay <u>rent</u> to the owner.

   <u>Rent</u> is money you pay to _____.

   a. own a house or an apartment   **b.** live in someone's house or apartment

10. I didn't have enough money for a new car, so I bought a <u>used</u> one. It's old, but it wasn't expensive.

    <u>Used</u> means _____.

    a. not expensive   **b.** not new

11. I have a lot of expenses, and I spend more money than I earn. I'm really in <u>debt</u>. To get out of debt, I need to earn more money or spend less money.

    To be in <u>debt</u> is to _____ money.

    a. owe   **b.** have

❷ *Cross out one word in each row that does not belong. Then compare your answers with a partner. Tell why you think each word doesn't belong. The first one has been done for you.*

1. ~~advisor~~	bill	payment	expense
2. credit cards	loans	cash	rent
3. house	car	spend	clothing
4. used	car	expensive	big

LISTENING ONE: Money Problems

A. INTRODUCING THE TOPIC

Listen to the beginning of the conversation. Then answer the questions.

1. What is Susan Anderson's job?

   a. a salesclerk   **b.** a money advisor   **c.** a bank teller

2. What do Henry and Carol Williams need to do?

   a. get jobs   **b.** get a loan   **c.** get out of debt

3. What do you think the listening will be about? Circle more than one answer.

   a. how to earn more money   **b.** how to save money
   c. how to use credit cards   **d.** how to buy a house
   e. how to make a budget

B. LISTENING FOR MAIN IDEAS

Listen to the conversation between a money management advisor and a couple who needs help getting out of debt. Circle the best answer to complete each sentence.

1. Susan Anderson thinks Henry and Carol should _____.

   a. earn more money   **b.** get a loan   **c.** spend less money

2. Henry and Carol's apartment is _____.

   a. beautiful and cheap   **b.** big and cheap   **c.** big and expensive

3. Henry's car is _____.

   a. expensive   **b.** small   **c.** old

4. Susan thinks Carol should _____.

   a. get more
      credit cards   **b.** stop using
         credit cards   **c.** keep only one
         credit card

5. The advisor tells Henry and Carol to write down their _____.

   a. expenses   **b.** income   **c.** budget

C. LISTENING FOR DETAILS

These are Susan's notes from her meeting with Henry and Carol. Listen to the conversation again. Fill in the missing information.

Clients: <u>Henry and Carol Williams</u>   Income: $_____ / month

CURRENT EXPENSES: ADVICE:

Rent: $_____ / month   • Get a cheaper apartment.

Car payments: $_____ / month • Buy a _____ car or take the _____.

Number of credit cards: _____   • Stop using them. Pay with _____.

Shopping and eating out: $ <u>don't know</u>   • Write down expenses for _____ weeks.

Now go back to Section 3A on page 37. Were your predictions correct?

D. LISTENING BETWEEN THE LINES

Listen to the excerpts from Listening One. Discuss these questions with the class.

Excerpt One

1. Does Carol like the apartment? Does Henry like the apartment? Why or why not?

2. Does the advisor think they should move? Why?

3. How does Carol feel about the advice? Will they move? Why or why not?

Excerpt Two

1. How does Susan think Henry should get to work?

2. How does Henry feel about her advice?

3. Why does Henry want to have an expensive car? Does the advisor think that's a good reason? Why or why not?

4. Do you think that's a good reason? Why or why not?

5. What does Carol think about Henry's car?

6. In your culture, who do people talk to about money problems? Who would you talk to if you had money problems?

4 LISTENING TWO: Saving Money

A. EXPANDING THE TOPIC

❶ *Look at the pictures and describe them. Then listen to the conversations. Circle the number of each conversation next to the correct picture in the chart.*

❷ *Listen again. What did the person buy? How much money did each person save? Write your answers in the chart.*

CONVERSATION	WHAT DID THE PERSON BUY?	HOW MUCH MONEY DID THE PERSON SAVE?
1 2 3		
1 2 3		
1 2 3		

Picture A

Picture B

Picture C

B. LINKING LISTENINGS ONE AND TWO

Work in a small group. Discuss the answers to these questions.

1. Do you prefer to spend your money or save your money? Why?

2. You have heard about some different ways to save money:

◆ make a budget   ◆ use coupons

◆ pay with cash   ◆ shop at factory outlet stores

◆ buy used things

Have you tried any of them? What do you think is the best way to save money? What do you think Henry and Carol should do to save money?

3. In your culture, is it polite to talk about the price of things? Who do you talk to about the price of things?

5 REVIEWING LANGUAGE

A. EXPLORING LANGUAGE: Numbers and Prices

When we say the numbers 13 through 19, the letter *t* in the second syllable *-teen* sounds like /t/. The second syllable is also usually stressed. When we say the numbers 20, 30, 40, 50, 60 ,70, 80, and 90, the letter *t* in the second syllable *-ty* sounds like /d/ and the first syllable is stressed.

Listen to these examples:

13	30
/thir<u>teen</u>/	/<u>thir</u>dy/

❶ *Listen to the numbers. Circle the number you hear.*

1. 13	30	**4.** 16	60	**6.** 18	80
2. 14	40	**5.** 17	70	**7.** 19	90
3. 15	50				

❷ *Work in pairs. Look at the numbers in Exercise 1 on page 40. Take turns. Say a number. Remember to stress the correct syllable. Your partner points to the number you say.*

❸ *There are two ways to say prices. Listen to these examples:*

$4.29   four dollars and twenty-nine cents
           four twenty-nine

$53.99   fifty-three dollars and ninety-nine cents
           fifty-three ninety-nine

Listen and write the prices you hear. Then practice saying them aloud in two different ways.

1. $_____

2. $_____

3. $_____

4. $_____

5. $_____

❹ *Work in pairs. Take turns asking each other how much you usually spend on the following expenses. Write down your partner's answers. Then compare your answers with the class.*

Example:
A: How much do you usually spend on a haircut?
B: I spend thirty dollars. How about you?
A: I only spend fifteen dollars.

1. a haircut $_____

2. a movie ticket $_____

3. a pair of shoes $_____

4. a meal in a restaurant $_____

B. WORKING WITH WORDS

1 *Work in pairs. Student A reads sentence A out loud. Student B reads sentence B with a word or phrase from the list. Both sentences should have the same meaning. Use the underlined words to help you. Switch roles after item 4. Check the answers in the Answer Key.*

cheap	pay interest	view
convenient	regular price	a waste of money
have enough	used	

1. A: I bought a chair at a thrift store yesterday. It <u>isn't new</u>, but it's very nice.

   B: You bought a _____ chair.

2. A: The chair <u>was inexpensive</u>.

   B: It was _____.

3. A: I <u>didn't have as much cash as I needed</u> to buy it, so I paid with a credit card.

   B: You didn't _____ cash with you.

4. A: I always buy clothes on sale. I never pay the <u>full price</u>.

   B: You never buy clothes at the _____

5. A: I live in a big apartment building. When I look out my window I <u>see a beautiful park</u>.

   B: You have a great _____.

6. A: I live downtown near my job and stores, and there's a bus stop in front of my house, too. It's <u>easy</u> for me to get anywhere.

   B: You live in a _____ location.

7. A: If you don't pay the credit card company all the money you owe them every month, you have to <u>pay extra money</u>.

   B: You have to _____.

8. A: Eating in restaurants <u>is not a good way to spend money</u>. I always eat at home.

   B: You think eating out is _____.

2 *Work in a small group. Take turns asking the questions. Each student in the group answers the questions. Use the underlined vocabulary in your answers.*

1. Do you live in a <u>convenient</u> location? Why is it or isn't it convenient?

2. Do you have a nice <u>view</u> from your house or apartment? What can you see?

3. Name something you own that was <u>cheap</u> to buy. How much did it cost?

4. Name something that you think is a <u>waste of money</u>. Why do you think it's a waste of money?

5. Describe a time when you didn't <u>have enough</u> cash to pay for something. What did you do?

6. How much <u>interest</u> do you usually pay on a credit card?

7. Do you usually buy things at the <u>regular price</u> or on sale? Why?

8. Do you like to buy things <u>used</u>? Why or why not? If yes, what are some things that you like to buy used? What are some things you never buy used?

SKILLS FOR EXPRESSION

A. GRAMMAR: Comparative Adjectives

1 *Read the sentences. Notice the underlined words. Then answer the questions below.*

♦ You need to find a <u>cheaper</u> place to live.

♦ Taking the bus is <u>slower</u> than driving.

a. What is the adjective in the first sentence? What does it describe? What two letters does the adjective end with?

b. What is the adjective in the second sentence? What does it describe? What word comes after *slower*?

Comparative Adjectives

Use the comparative form of the adjective to compare two people, places, or things.

a. Add *-er* to form the comparative of short (one-syllable) adjectives. Use *than* before the person or thing you are comparing.

   ◆ Used clothing is **older than** new clothing.

b. When a one-syllable adjective ends in a consonant, double the last consonant and add *-er.*

   ◆ A bus is **bigger than** a car.

c. To form the comparative of most adjectives of two or more syllables, add *more* before the adjective.

   ◆ Credit cards are **more expensive than** cash.

d. When two-syllable adjectives end in *-y,* change the *y* to *i* and add *-er.*

   ◆ Using a credit card is **easier than** paying with cash.

e. *Less* is the opposite of *more.*

   ◆ Taking the bus is **less convenient than** driving.

f. Some comparative forms are irregular: The comparative of *good* is *better.*

   ◆ My new car is **better than** the old one.

g. The comparative form of *bad* is *worse.*

   ◆ Your apartment is **worse than** mine.

big

expensive

old

nice

comfortable

easy to park

safe

bad for the environment

cheap to drive

good for a big family

❷ *Work in pairs. Look at the ads for the cars. Take turns making sentences comparing the two cars. Use the adjectives on the left. Then decide which car you would like to buy, and say why.*

Example:

A: The Indulge is bigger than the Pee Wee.

B: The Indulge is more expensive than the Pee Wee.

Introducing the new
INDULGE

Buy a new
Indulge and
drive in comfort,
style, and safety for only $40,000!

This week's special: a used
Pee Wee

This *Pee Wee*
is old but it runs
well! It gets great
gas mileage and it's on sale now for only $1,000!

❸ *Write ten sentences comparing the Indulge and the Pee Wee. Read them to the class.*

B. STYLE: Shopping Language—Asking for and Refusing Help

When shopping, you may or may not want help. There are useful expressions to ask a salesclerk for help, or to refuse help when a salesclerk offers it.

Asking for help:

Could you help me?   Do you have this (these) in a size 8?
                                                        in blue?

How much is this?

How much does this cost?   Can I try this (these) on?

- -

Offering help:	**Refusing:**	**Buying something:**
May I help you?	No, I'm just looking, thanks.	I'd like to buy this (these).
Would you like to buy it?	I'll think about it.	Yes, I'll take it (them).
	I'll come back later.	

---

❶ *Complete the following conversations. Then practice them out loud with a partner.*

1. A: May _____?

   B: Yes, _____ these shoes in a size 7?

   A: Yes, I'll be right back.

   B: Thank you.

2. A: Could _____?

   B: Yes, what would you like?

   A: _____ this TV cost?

   B: It's $895. Would you _____?

   A: _____.

3. A: May I help you?

   B: No, _____.

❷ *Work with another student. Think of something you'd like to buy. Student A is a salesclerk in a store who offers help. Student B is a shopper who asks for help and buys something. Then change roles. Student B is a salesclerk who offers help. Student A is a shopper who refuses help. Use the shopping language from the box on page 45. Then perform one of your conversations for the class.*

Listening Task

The class answers the following questions.

What kind of store are they in?
Does the shopper buy anything?
If yes, what is it? How much does it cost?

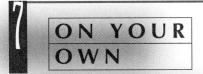

ON YOUR OWN

A. SPEAKING TOPICS: Having a Debate

❶ *Prepare for a debate. Work in a small group. Take turns comparing the pairs of items in the list. Say which one you think is better and explain why. Then think of two more things to compare.*

Example:

A: I think cash is better than credit cards because you don't have to pay interest on cash.

B: I think credit cards are better than cash because they're safer. It's more dangerous to carry cash because someone can steal it.

1. cash / credit cards

2. taking the bus / driving a car

3. used cars / new cars

4. rent / house payments

5. department stores / thrift stores

6. eating at home / eating out

7. asking an advisor for advice / asking your family for advice

8. going into debt for a house / going into debt for clothing

_____

_____

2 *Share your answers with the class. How many differences can you think of?*

3 *Have a debate. Follow the steps below.*

Step 1: Work in groups of six. Choose one of the pairs of items in exercise 1 on page 46. Three students in the group agree on one opinion and the other three agree on the opposite opinion. For example, half the group thinks, "Paying with cash is better than paying with credit cards," and the other half thinks, "Paying with credit cards is better than paying with cash."

Step 2: Now work with only the students that have the same opinion. Write your opinion below. Then make a list of all of your reasons to support your opinion. Everyone in the group should have a chance to speak.

Our opinion: _____

_____

Our reasons: _____

_____

_____

_____

_____

_____

_____

_____

Step 3: Have a debate with the whole group.

Listening Task

The rest of the class listens.

Who has the best reasons?

B. FIELDWORK

Before most Americans buy something, especially something expensive, they do comparison shopping. They compare the different choices and then decide which is the best one to buy.

Think of something you would like to buy, such as a camera, a television, or a new jacket. Then go to a store and compare two different kinds. Use polite shopping language to ask a salesclerk for help. Answer the following questions about your choice:

1. How much does it cost?

2. What does it look like?

3. How well is it made?

4. How big is it?

5. Is it what I need?

6. Why is it better than the other one?

Report back to the class telling which one you would like to buy and why.

Listening Task

The class answers these questions:

1. Do you agree with the choice? Why or why not?

2. Which item would you like to buy?

AT YOUR SERVICE:
SERVICE ANIMALS

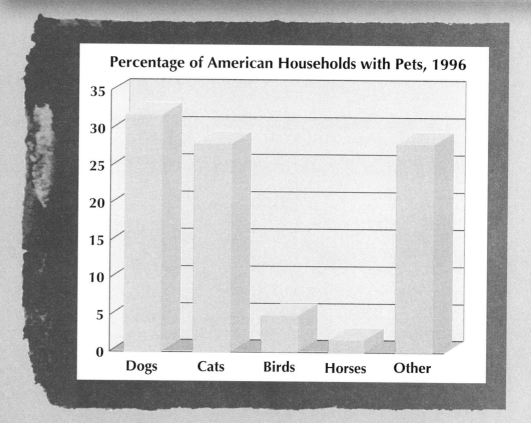

Percentage of American Households with Pets, 1996

APPROACHING THE TOPIC

A. PREDICTING

Look at the graph. Discuss these questions with the class.

1. What animals did Americans own in 1996?
2. Which animal was most popular? Why?
3. What are "other pets"?
4. Why do people own these different animals?
5. Look at the title of the unit. What do you think service animals are?

B. SHARING INFORMATION

Work in groups of four. Write the names of the students in your group. Discuss the questions in the chart and write each student's answers. Then one student will report to the class.

Example: "Three people have pets, and one person doesn't have pets."

NAMES				
1. Do you have any pets now? What kinds of pets do you have?				
2. If you don't have pets now, did you ever have pets? What kinds of pets did you have?				
3. Are pets popular in your home culture? What kinds of pets are popular in your home culture?				

Listen to all the reports and answer these questions.

1. How many people in the class have pets?

2. Which pets are the most popular?

3. Why do you think these pets are the most popular?

PREPARING TO LISTEN

A. BACKGROUND

Read the paragraph. Then follow the directions.

Many people have animals. Animals can be pets. Pets are friends or companions to people. But some animals are also service animals. Service animals are animals that do work.

Work with a partner. Look at the animals listed in the far left column and the kinds of work listed below. Which animals can do the work? Write the names of the animals. You can use the animals in the list or think of others. Then compare your answers with the class.

Animals	Work	Animals
bird	Work on a farm	*donkey, horse, cow*
cat	Move heavy things	
cow	Move people from place to place	
dog	Bring information to people	
donkey	Help find lost people	
horse	Help people who can't see	
	Help people who can't hear	
	Help people feel safe	

B. VOCABULARY FOR COMPREHENSION

Read the paragraphs. Guess the meanings of the underlined words. Then match each word with its definition. Write the number of the word in the blank on page 52.

Many people have dogs as pets. Dogs can be friends to their owners. They like to be with their (1) <u>owners</u> and follow them around. Some dogs are more than pets; they are service dogs. Service dogs can (2) <u>assist</u>, or help, their owners in different ways. For example, some service dogs assist owners who can't see. They help their owners cross the street and get from place to place. Some service dogs assist people who are (3) <u>deaf</u>. These dogs are called (4) <u>hearing dogs</u>. Hearing dogs hear (5) <u>sounds</u> such as (6) <u>alarms</u>. Alarms ring to tell people there is an emergency, but deaf people can't hear the alarms. The hearing dogs tell deaf people about sounds by (7) <u>getting their attention</u>. Hearing dogs must make deaf people look at them. To get someone's attention, they touch the person.

Service dogs go to special schools and are (8) <u>trained</u> to help people. By assisting their owners, service dogs help their owners feel (9) <u>safe</u>. In fact, in emergencies, service dogs can really (10) <u>save someone's life</u>. They can protect a person from danger.

_____ **a.** things you hear

_____ **b.** dogs that assist deaf people

_____ **c.** taught

_____ **d.** people who have something

_____ **e.** noises made in emergencies

_____ **f.** making a person look at you

_____ **g.** protect someone from danger

_____ **h.** help

_____ **i.** not hurt or in danger

_____ **j.** can't hear

3 LISTENING ONE: Kimba, the Hero Dog

A. INTRODUCING THE TOPIC

Read the questions. Listen to the first part of "Kimba, the Hero Dog." Then answer the questions.

1. What are you listening to?

   a. a telephone conversation   **b.** a news report   **c.** an interview

2. Where is the woman who is speaking?

   a. at a fire   **b.** in the newsroom   **c.** at her house

3. What do you think she is going to talk about? Circle more than one answer.

   a. people and dogs in general   **b.** fires and dogs   **c.** a special dog that helped someone

   d. the fire department   **e.** the food dogs eat   **f.** how dogs help people

B. LISTENING FOR MAIN IDEAS

Listen to the news report. Which of the following questions are answered? Check (✓) the ones you hear.

_____ 1. What happened at the fire?

_____ 2. How do firefighters put out fires?

_____ 3. What do hearing dogs do?

_____ 4. How do people hear?

_____ 5. Why do people use hearing dogs?

_____ 6. How do hearing dogs tell deaf people about sounds?

_____ 7. Where do deaf people use hearing dogs?

C. LISTENING FOR DETAILS

*Listen to the news report again. Read the sentences. Write **T** for the sentences that are true and **F** for the sentences that are false.*

_____ 1. Mrs. Ravenscroft's dog, Kimba, is deaf.

_____ 2. The fire started in the living room.

_____ 3. Mrs. Ravenscroft saved Kimba's life.

_____ 4. Hearing dogs tell deaf people about many sounds.

_____ 5. We don't think about sounds because they're not important.

_____ 6. First, the hearing dog goes to the deaf person and then to the sound.

_____ 7. Hearing dogs cannot go into restaurants and stores.

_____ 8. Hearing dogs are also companions.

_____ 9. After the fire, Mrs. Ravenscroft called Kimba her personal hero dog.

Now go back to Section 3A on page 52. Were your predictions correct?

D. LISTENING BETWEEN THE LINES

Work in pairs. Listen to the excerpts from Listening One. Then answer these questions.

Excerpt One

1 What are some sounds hearing dogs tell deaf people about?

2. How do you think hearing dogs are trained?

3. Do you think you'd like to train hearing dogs? Why or why not?

Excerpt Two

1. Where do deaf people take their hearing dogs?

2. Why do you think deaf people take hearing dogs into restaurants and stores with them?

3. Imagine you are in a restaurant or a store and someone comes in with a hearing dog. How would you feel about it? What would you think? Why?

4 LISTENING TWO: Do People Help Animals, Too?

A. EXPANDING THE TOPIC

❶ *Describe the picture with your class. What do you see?*

❷ *Work with a partner. Before you listen to "Do People Help Animals, Too?" look at the picture again and try to answer the questions. Write short answers. Then listen and check your answers.*

	BEFORE YOU LISTEN	AFTER YOU LISTEN
1. Where is the dog?		
2. Who are the people standing on the street?		
3. Why is the truck there?		

 ❸ *Listen again and answer these questions with your partner.*

1. How does the woman feel about saving the dog? How does the man feel?

2. Who do you agree with, the man or the woman? Why?

B. LINKING LISTENINGS ONE AND TWO

In this unit, you learned about a dog who helped someone. You also learned about some people who helped a dog. Animals are important to people, and people are important to animals, too.

❶ *On a separate piece of paper, make two lists. What are some things animals do for people? What are some things people do for animals?*

❷ *Are animals important to people in your culture? How are they important?*

5 REVIEWING LANGUAGE

A. EXPLORING LANGUAGE: Intonation

When we ask wh- questions (*what, when, where, who, why*) we use falling intonation. Our voice gets lower, or falls, at the end of a wh- question.

Listen.

◆ What do service animals do?

◆ What does a hearing dog do?

◆ Where do hearing dogs go?

❶ *Listen to the questions. Draw an arrow over each question to show falling intonation. Then practice asking the questions.*

1. What do service animals do?

2. What do hearing dogs do?

3. Where do deaf people use hearing dogs?

4. Why do deaf people use hearing dogs?

5. What do you think about hearing dogs?

❷ *Work in pairs. Student A asks the questions from Exercise 1 using falling intonation. Student B answers the questions about the story in Listening One. Then change roles.*

B. WORKING WITH WORDS

Work in pairs. Fill in the blanks in the conversation using the words and phrases below. Use the underlined words to help you. Then practice the conversation out loud with your partner. Take turns reading each part.

caught on fire	hero	saved
companion	owns	service dog
get her attention	safe	trained

A: Have you read the newspaper today?

B: No. What happened?

A: Well, do you know the woman who lives nearby? You know, she has a <u>special dog that works for people</u>.

B: Yeah. She has a (**1**) _____ _____.

A: Right. Well, she was home and <u>there was a fire</u> at her house.

B: Really? Her house (**2**) _____ _____ _____?

A: Yeah. But <u>no one was hurt</u>. Everyone got out of the house.

B: Good. I'm glad everyone was (**3**) _____.

A: Do you know how her dog <u>told her about the fire</u>?

B: No. How did the dog (**4**) _____ _____ _____?

A: Well, the dog ran back and forth to the kitchen. Then the woman looked and saw the fire. Someone really <u>taught</u> that dog well.

B: Service dogs are (**5**) _____ to help in emergencies.

A: It's good she <u>has</u> a service dog.

B: I'm sure she is happy she (**6**) _____ one.

A: That dog is really a good <u>friend</u>.

B: Yeah. Her service dog is a great (**7**) _____.

A: And the dog did a great thing! He <u>protected her from danger</u>.

B: He sure did. He (**8**) _____ her life!

A: He did a wonderful thing.

B: Yeah. He's a (**9**) _____!

SKILLS FOR EXPRESSION

A. GRAMMAR: Simple Present Tense—Wh- Questions with *Do*

❶ *Read the examples from the news report in Listening One. Then answer the questions below.*

- ◆ What does a hearing dog do?
- ◆ Where do they go?
- ◆ Why do people use hearing dogs?

a. What is the first word in each sentence? What kind of answer do you expect?

b. Underline the verbs. How many verbs are there in each sentence? What's the form of the second verb?

FOCUS ON GRAMMAR

See Simple Present Tense—Wh- Questions with *Do* in *Focus on Grammar, Basic.*

Wh- Questions with *Do*

Use *do* or *does* with wh- words: ◆ To ask questions in the present tense using verbs other than *be*	Where **do** hearing dogs **go?** Why **does** a deaf person **own** a hearing dog?
To form wh- questions with *do:* ◆ Use a wh- word and the base form of the verb. Wh- words are **what, where, when, who,** and **why**	What animals **do** they train?
◆ Use *do* with *I, you,* and *they*	Why **do I** own a cat? Where **do you** play with your dog? When **do they** use hearing dogs?
◆ Use *does* with *he, she,* or *it*	Why **does she** own a hearing dog? When **does it** go to the door? Who(m) **does he** call about hearing dogs?

② *Work in pairs. Look at the picture. Take turns asking and answering questions. Use question words.*

Example: Student A: Where does the woman work?
　　　　　 Student B: She works in the circus.

1. Where / the woman work?

2. What / the woman do every day at work?

3. Where / the lion live?

4. Who / the lion live with?

5. Where / lions usually live?

6. What / lions usually do all day?

7. When / lions sleep?

8. What / lions eat?

9. Why / you think people like to watch circus animals?

10. What / you think about circus animals?

B. STYLE: Asking for More Information

A good way to keep a conversation going is to ask follow-up questions. Follow-up questions give you more information.

❶ *Read the conversation. The follow-up questions are underlined.*

A: I like pets.

B: Really. That's interesting. <u>What pets do you like?</u>

A: Well, I like cats. How about you?

B: I like cats, too. <u>Why do you like cats?</u>

A: Oh, cats are so friendly!

B: I agree. <u>Do you have cats?</u>

A: Yes, I have three.

B: Three cats! Wow! You really do like cats. <u>What are their names?</u>

A: Well, they are Tikos, Nikos, and Mikos.

❷ *Read the statements. Circle an appropriate follow-up question. Then practice the conversation out loud with another student.*

1. A: I own a pet.

   B: **a.** What pet do you own?

   b. Where do you live?

2. A: I own a dog.

   B: **a.** What is your dog's name?

   b. What pets do you like?

3. A: Her name is Blue.

   B: **a.** That's a nice name. Does she like to play?

   b. Do you like dogs?

4. A: Oh, yes. She loves to play. She's a great companion, too.

   B: **a.** Where do you go with her?

   b. Why is she a good companion?

5. A: She's trained to help me.

   B: **a.** What does she do?

   b. Why do you have a dog?

6. A: She assists me on the farm.

   B: **a.** Where is your farm?

   b. What does she do?

   A: Oh, she does many things. Usually, she helps me with the other animals.

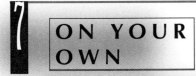

ON YOUR OWN

A. SPEAKING TOPICS: Discussing Animal Issues

In this unit you learned about animals as pets and as service animals. But animals are also used for food, clothing, and science. Many people disagree about the different uses of animals.

Step 1: *Work in groups of four. Read the four topics for discussion on pages 61–63. Read the example discussion question. Then make wh- questions with all of the phrases listed for each topic.*

Step 2: *Each group chooses one topic to discuss. The leader will read the questions and the students in the group should discuss each question.*

Topic 1: Vegetarians and Vegans

Some people are vegetarians. They don't eat meat. Other people are vegans. They don't eat or use anything made of animals—this includes clothing and food.

Example: Why do people use animals for food?

1. Why
   ◆ people use animals for food
   ◆ people use animals for clothing like shoes and coats

2. What
   ◆ vegetarians eat
   ◆ vegans eat
   ◆ vegans use for shoes or clothing

3. Why
   ◆ you think some people are vegetarians
   ◆ you think some people are vegans

Topic 2: Fur Coats

You are going shopping and you see people standing in front of the store with signs that say, *Don't buy from this store—they sell fur coats. Cruelty to animals!*

1. Why

    ◆ people make fur coats

    ◆ people own fur coats

    ◆ some people not like fur coats

2. What animals

    ◆ people use to make fur coats

3. What

    ◆ you think about fur coats

Topic 3: Animal Testing

Often scientists use animals to test new medicines. They want to know if the medicine is safe for people to use. Also, companies that manufacture make-up or other health and beauty products use animals to test the products to see if they are safe for people. This is called animal testing.

1. Why

    ◆ people use animals to test products

    ◆ people not like animal testing

2. What

    ◆ scientists do during animal testing

3. Where

    ◆ animals that are used for testing live

4. What

    ◆ you think about animal testing

Topic 4: Pets

Pets are popular in the United States. Many people let their pets live in the house and even sleep on the bed. They treat their pets like children. When the pets are sick, people spend a lot of money to make them healthy again.

1. Where
   - pets live in your country

2. What
   - people in your country do with sick animals

3. Why
   - people spend money to help a sick pet

4. What
   - you think about pets sleeping on the bed
   - you think about spending a lot of money to help a sick pet

B. FIELDWORK

Dogs that help deaf people are just one kind of service animal. There are many others. Blind people use Seeing Eye dogs. Some people who use wheelchairs have dogs to help them get things or open doors, and some dogs are companions for people with medical problems such as depression. Service animals can also help people in their work. For example, horses and donkeys work on farms.

Find out about another service animal. You can go to the library and find a book, look on the Internet, or find an organization that trains special animals. Use the questions on page 64 to help you organize information. You can add other questions. Then tell the class what you learned.

Questions about Service Animals

◆ What is the animal?

◆ What does the animal do?

◆ Where does the animal live?

◆ What does the animal eat?

◆ Who does the animal help?

◆ Why do people use the animal?

◆ When do people use the animal?

◆ Where do people use the animal?

Listening Task

Pick one presentation you liked. Write the answers to the questions about the animal.

SURFING IN THE SKY

1 APPROACHING THE TOPIC

A. PREDICTING

Look at the picture. Read the title of the unit. Discuss the answers to these questions with the class.

1. What sports do you see in the picture?
2. What sports do you like?
3. What do you think the title of the unit means?

B. SHARING INFORMATION

Work in a small group. Write your answers to the questions about each of the sports below. Then compare your answers with the class.

Sport	Is it a team or an individual sport?	Is it an indoor or an outdoor sport?	Is it popular in your home culture?	Why do you think people like the sport?
1. skydiving	_____	_____	_____	_____
2. bungee jumping	_____	_____	_____	_____
3. gymnastics	_____	_____	_____	_____
4. skiing	_____	_____	_____	_____
5. surfing	_____	_____	_____	_____

2 PREPARING TO LISTEN

A. BACKGROUND

Look at the list of sports. Which sports do you think are dangerous and which sports do you think are safe? Rank the sports on a scale from 1 to 10. Write the numbers in the blanks. Then compare your answers in a small group. Explain your answers.

10	9	8	7	6	5	4	3	2	1
very dangerous			dangerous			safe		very safe	

_____ skydiving   _____ bungee jumping   _____ surfing

_____ skiing   _____ hang gliding   _____ swimming

_____ gymnastics   _____ diving   _____ basketball

B. VOCABULARY FOR COMPREHENSION

Read the paragraphs. Then use the underlined words to complete the sentences.

Are you the kind of person who likes dangerous sports? If so, maybe skydiving is for you. Not only is it dangerous, but it's exciting. First, sky divers <u>jump</u> from an airplane. Then, sky divers <u>fall</u> quickly toward the ground. Sometimes, sky divers do gymnastics in the air—for example, they might hold their knees close to their bodies and turn upside down. This is called a <u>flip</u>. Finally, sky divers pull a cord and a <u>parachute</u> opens. The parachute helps slow the sky diver so he or she lands on the ground safely. Sky divers usually wear hard <u>helmets</u> on their heads. The helmets protect them so they don't get hurt. Sometimes, sky divers are on a <u>team</u> in a competition such as the Olympics. The team works together and does movements in the air. <u>Judges</u> watch the sky divers and give them <u>points</u> for doing amazing things. The team with the most points wins.

It's difficult to see what sky divers do when you're standing on the ground. Often, people fly in airplanes to make a tape of the sky divers with a video camera. The <u>video camera operator</u> makes the tape of the sky divers.

If jumping out of airplanes doesn't sound like fun to you, there are plenty of other sports. You can always try surfing. <u>Surfers</u> stand out in the middle of the ocean on a long, flat <u>board</u>. Surfers don't have to worry about jumping out of airplanes, of course—but don't forget about the sharks!

1. _____ watch sports competitions. They give _____ to the athletes.

2. Basketball, soccer, and football are examples of _____ sports.

3. The first thing sky divers do is _____ from an airplane. Then they _____ quickly. Sometimes they do a _____ or other gymnastics. Sky divers use special equipment to help them slow down. They use a _____.

4. A person who uses a video camera to tape a sports competition is called a _____ _____ _____.

5. _____ stand out in the middle of the ocean on a long, flat _____.

LISTENING ONE: The Competition

A. INTRODUCING THE TOPIC

❶ *Work with a partner. Look at the photograph. What is the man doing?*

❷ *Listen to the tape with a partner. You will hear two reporters describing a sports competition. Look at the list below and check (✓) everything you think you will hear about.*

_____ sports in general   _____ flying in airplanes

_____ getting points   _____ rules for this sport

_____ clothing for this sport   _____ people who participate in
                                                          this sport

B. LISTENING FOR MAIN IDEAS

*Listen to the two reporters describe a sky-surfing competition. Read the sentences. Write **T** for the sentences that are true and **F** for the sentences that are false.*

_____ **1.** Anna Lee and Jerry Daniels are watching a sports competition on TV.

_____ **2.** There are two people on a sky-surfing team.

_____ **3.** One person on the team goes in the airplane.

_____ **4.** Michelle and Mike both jump from the airplane.

_____ **5.** The judges don't watch the videotape.

C. LISTENING FOR DETAILS

Read each sentence. Then listen to "The Competition" again. Circle the best answer to complete each sentence.

1. Surfers who jump from airplanes are _____.

   a. sky divers   **b.** sky surfers

2. The team gets _____ for good gymnastics and good sky surfing.

   a. points   **b.** a videotape

3. A sky board costs more than _____.

   a. $1,600.00   **b.** $600.00

4. Mike is putting the video camera _____.

   a. in his backpack   **b.** on his helmet

5. The plane is going to _____.

   a. 15,000 feet   **b.** 13,000 feet

6. Sky surfers fall _____ miles per hour.

   a. 130   **b.** 120

7. The parachute opens at _____ feet.

   a. 5,000   **b.** 9,000

8. _____ is going sky surfing.

   a. Anna   **b.** Jerry

Now go back to Section 3A on page 68. Were your predictions correct?

D. LISTENING BETWEEN THE LINES

Listen to Jerry talking. How does he feel? Check (✓) the correct emotions on the chart on page 70. Write the reason for your answer. Then discuss the reason with your class.

	WORRIED	EXCITED	RELIEVED	WHY DO YOU THINK HE FEELS THIS WAY?
Excerpt One				
Excerpt Two				
Excerpt Three				
Excerpt Four				

4 LISTENING TWO: Other Sports

A. EXPANDING THE TOPIC

❶ *Look at the sports listed in Exercise 2 below. Discuss the questions with a partner.*

1. Where do people participate in each of the sports?

2. What do you think people like about each of the sports?

❷ *Now listen to the people talk about things they like to do. Match their names to a sport they might like.*

Annabelle	bungee jumping
Louis	surfing
Susan	hang gliding
Mark	skiing

B. LINKING LISTENINGS ONE AND TWO

Discuss these questions with the class.

1. Look at the list of sports. Check the ones you have tried.

_____ skiing   _____ sky surfing   _____ hang gliding

_____ surfing   _____ bungee jumping

2. What other dangerous sports do you know about?

3. Do you want to try a dangerous sport? Which one? Why?

4. What sports do you enjoy? Why?

REVIEWING LANGUAGE

A. EXPLORING LANGUAGE: Pronunciation

In speaking, we often use contractions. Contractions are short forms. They join two words together.

Contractions

		Affirmative Contractions	Negative Contractions	
I am		I'm	I'm not	
He is		He's	He's not / He isn't	
She is	jumping.	She's	She's not / She isn't	jumping.
We are		We're	We're not / We aren't	
They are		They're	They're not / They aren't	
You are		You're	You're not / You aren't	

❶ *Listen to each sentence. Write **A** if it is affirmative and **N** if it is negative. Then listen again and write the sentences on a separate piece of paper.*

1. _____   2. _____   3. _____   4. _____   5. _____

❷ *Work with a partner. Student A reads a sentence from column 1 or 2. Column 1 has contractions. Column 2 doesn't have contractions. Student B listens and points to the corresponding sentence. Listen carefully. Then switch.*

Column 1

She's sky surfing.

They're watching a team.

He's videotaping.

We're jumping from an airplane.

I'm not sky surfing.

They aren't smiling.

Column 2

She is sky surfing.

They are watching a team.

He is videotaping.

We are jumping from an airplane.

I am not sky surfing

They are not smiling.

B. WORKING WITH WORDS

❶ *Work with a partner. Each of the words and phrases below goes with one of the verbs in the chart. Some words and phrases can go with more than one verb. Complete the chart. Then think of two more words to add to each column.*

| afraid of heights | a board | brave | downhill | points |
| a helmet | on a team | outdoors | a parachute | ready |

BE	GET	GO	WEAR	USE
outdoors		outdoors		

2 *Work in a small group. Ask and answer these questions. One student asks one question of each student in the group. Each student answers. Then the next student asks the next question of each student in the group. Continue until all the questions are answered.*

1. How do you get ready to participate in your favorite sport?

2. Describe a brave person you know. Why is he or she brave?

3. Are you ever afraid of heights? When?

4. How do sky surfers get points?

5. What do you like to do outdoors?

6. Have you ever been on a team? Describe it.

SKILLS FOR EXPRESSION

A. GRAMMAR: Present Progressive

1 *Read the conversation. Underline the verbs. Then discuss the questions with the class.*

A: We are watching a sky-surfing competition.
B: What is happening?
A: They are jumping from an airplane.
B: Are they falling fast?
A: Yes, they are!

a. Are the people talking about watching a competition now, in the future, or in the past?

b. What verbs did you underline? How many parts do the verbs have?

c. What do you notice about the ending of the verbs?

See Present Progressive in *Focus on Grammar, Basic.*

FOCUS ON GRAMMAR

Present Progressive	
Use the present progressive: ◆ To talk about an event that is happening now, as you are speaking	We **are watching** (we**'re watching**) a sky-surfing competition. Michelle and Mike are getting ready to sky surf.
To form the present progressive: ◆ Use **be** + the base form of the verb + **-ing**	I **am jumping**. / I**'m jumping**. He **is falling**. / He**'s falling.** They **are sky surfing**. / They**'re sky surfing.**
To form a negative: ◆ Add **not** after the **be** verb (notice the contractions)	I **am not doing** gymnastics. I**'m not doing** gymnastics. She**'s not wearing** a helmet. She **isn't wearing** a helmet. They**'re not jumping**. They **aren't jumping**.
To form *yes/no* questions: ◆ Use **be** + subject + base form of the verb + **-ing**	**Are you sky surfing?** **Is she smiling?**
To form wh- questions: ◆ Use a wh- word at the beginning of the question	**Where** are you going? **When** is the plane taking off?

❷ *Work in pairs. Practice affirmative and negative statements with the present progressive. Student A describes one thing that is happening in one of the pictures on page 75. Student B points to the correct picture. Then switch. How many sentences can you make about each picture?*

Example: Student A: They're sky surfing. (Picture 2)
Student B: They're talking to each other. (Picture 1)

Picture 1   Picture 2   Picture 3

3 **Part A:** *Look at the groups of words. Each group describes a different sport. Work with a partner or in a small group. Write the name of the sport. Add more vocabulary words to each sport if you can.*

a. <u>Sky surfing</u>   b. _____   c. _____

use a parachute	jump	run
wear a helmet	wear a helmet	flip
fall	bounce	get points
jump	use a bungee cord	stretch
wear goggles	fall	turn
turn	scream	
flip		

d. _____   e. _____

ride waves	go downhill
wear a bathing suit	wear goggles
wear a wet suit	wear warm clothes
	take a ski lift

Part B: *Work in groups of four. One student thinks of a sport and imagines doing the sport now. The other students each ask* **yes/no** *and* **wh-** *questions to guess the sport. They use the present progressive. Look at Part A above for vocabulary.*

Example:

A: I'm thinking of a sport.   A: No, I'm not.

B: Are you inside?   B: Are you riding a wave?

A: No, I'm not.   A: Yes, I am.

C: Where are you?   C: Are you surfing?

A: I'm outside.   A: Yes, I am!

D: Are you falling?

B. STYLE: Expressing Likes and Dislikes

We can use different phrases to express likes and dislikes.

Expressing Likes	Expressing Dislikes
What do you think about sky surfing? ◆ I **like** sky surfing. ◆ I **really like** sky surfing. ◆ I **think** sky surfing's **great**! ◆ **It's my favorite** sport. ◆ I **love** sky surfing!	What do you think about sky surfing? ◆ Sky surfing is **OK**. ◆ Sky surfing is **all right**. ◆ **I'm not crazy about** sky surfing. ◆ **I don't really like** sky surfing. ◆ **I can't stand** sky surfing. ◆ **I hate** sky surfing.

Write the names of three sports in the chart. Then ask four students what they think of the sports. Write their opinions. Use these questions:

a. How do you like . . . ?   **b.** What do you think about . . . ?

SPORTS	STUDENT 1	STUDENT 2	STUDENT 3	STUDENT 4
Example: basketball	She loves it.	He thinks it's OK.	He's not crazy about it.	It's her favorite sport.
1.				
2.				
3.				

Now choose one student and tell the class about him or her.

ON YOUR OWN

A. SPEAKING TOPICS: Role Play

Work with another student. Imagine you are announcers at an event. Follow the steps below.

Step 1: *Choose an event. Look at the list, or think of a new one.*

a fashion show   a basketball game

a dog/cat/horse show   a soccer game

a gymnastics tournament   _____

Step 2: *Make a list of all the verbs to describe the event and the information to include in the role play.*

> ### Information to Include When You Describe the Event
>
> Location: Where are you?
>
> People: Who is there?
>
> Activities: What's happening? What are you watching?
>
> Other information about the sport or event: For example, cost, equipment, clothing

Step 3: *Practice announcing the event. One student can ask questions and the other can answer them. Be sure to use the present progressive (see Section 6A) and phrases to express likes and dislikes (see Section 6B).*

Example:

Student A: Hi, I'm _____.

Student B: And I'm_____.

Student A: We're here telling you about this exciting event.

Student B: There are <u>twenty people</u>. They are <u>standing on a field</u>.

Student A: And they are all wearing <u>the same clothes. They are wearing shorts and T-shirts</u>.

Step 4: *Perform your role play for the class. Don't say the name of the event. The other students in the class must guess where you are and what you are watching.*

B. FIELDWORK

Choose an unusual sport. Choose one from the list below, or think of another. Go to the library and find a book or a magazine. Look in an encyclopedia or on the Internet. Find a picture, a videotape, or an article about the sport. Describe the sport to your class. Answer these questions in your description.

◆ Where do people participate in the sport?

◆ Is it dangerous? Why or why not?

◆ What equipment do you need for the sport?

◆ Is it expensive? How much does it cost?

◆ Do both men and women participate in the sport?

Unusual Sports

mud wrestling	snowboarding	dogsledding
parasailing	ultimate Frisbee	curling
rock climbing	white-water rafting	bobsledding

Listening Task

Choose one presentation you liked and answer the questions above. Write your answers on a separate piece of paper. Then write one sentence explaining why you chose that presentation.

IS IT WOMEN'S WORK?

1 APPROACHING THE TOPIC

A. PREDICTING

Look at the picture. Read the title of the unit. Discuss these questions with the class.

1. Point to the people in the picture. What activities do you see? Who is doing each activity?

2. Look at the title of the unit. What do you think the unit will be about?

B. SHARING INFORMATION

Work in groups of four. Look at the chart. Write the names of the students in your group. Each student says who in his or her household usually does the different household chores (for example, mother, father, son, daughter, grandmother, grandfather, both mother and father, and so on). Discuss the questions in the chart about your household and write each student's answers. When you are finished, discuss the questions that follow the chart.

NAMES	WHO COOKS?	WHO CLEANS?	WHO REPAIRS THINGS?	WHO TAKES CARE OF CHILDREN?	WHO MANAGES MONEY / PAYS BILLS?

1. What do men usually do?

2. What do women usually do?

3. What do both men and women do equally? Why?

2 PREPARING TO LISTEN

A. BACKGROUND

Read the paragraph. Then follow the directions below.

One important chore in households with children is taking care of the children. In some households, family members take care of the children. In other households, families want additional help, so they use child care. They hire people to take care of their children.

1 *Look at the list. Imagine you need child care. Rank the things to consider when choosing child care in order of importance from 1 (most important) to 11 (least important).*

_____ The child care is cheap.

_____ It's convenient (near my work or home).

_____ The child-care worker is friendly and caring with children.

_____ The child-care worker is female.

_____ The child-care worker is male.

_____ The child-care worker speaks my language.

_____ The child-care worker is from my culture.

_____ The child-care worker has experience.

_____ The child-care worker has training, for example, he or she studied child care in school.

_____ The child-care worker is someone I know, not a stranger.

_____ The child-care worker is my relative.

2 *Now compare your answers in a group. Tell why each item is important or not important to you.*

B. VOCABULARY FOR COMPREHENSION

Read the paragraphs. Guess the meanings of the underlined words. Then match each word with its definition. Write the number of the word in the blank.

Families all over the world are different—there is no (1) <u>typical</u> family. In different families, men and women sometimes do different (2) <u>household chores</u> such as cooking and cleaning. But, there is one question all families with children have: Who takes care of the children when the parents work? Who does the (3) <u>child care</u>?

There are a few choices for working parents. One choice is to take the children to a day-care center. Parents can bring their children to the day-care center before work and pick them up after work. Another choice is to (4) <u>hire</u> a (5) <u>sitter</u> whose job it is to take care of children. A sitter may take care of children in his or her house or come to the family's house. Another choice is to hire a (6) <u>nanny</u>. A nanny usually lives with a family and takes care of the children. Sometimes (7) <u>child-care workers</u> go to school where they get (8) <u>training</u> in taking care of children.

_____ **a.** a person who takes care of children in the family's home or in his or her home

_____ **b.** give a job to

_____ **c.** education to learn how to do something

_____ **d.** work in the house such as cooking and cleaning

_____ **e.** people who take care of children

_____ **f.** a person who usually lives with a family and takes care of the children

_____ **g.** usual or regular

_____ **h.** taking care of children while parents work

3 LISTENING ONE: Who's Taking Care of the Children?

A. INTRODUCING THE TOPIC

You are going to listen to an interview on a TV talk show. Listen to the introduction. Then answer the questions.

1. What is the talk show about?

    a. men and women

    b. child care

    c. children

2. Who is Julie Jones going to interview?

    a. a parent

    b. a nanny

    c. a young child

3. What are three questions you think Julie Jones will ask?

    a. _____

    b. _____

    c. _____

B. LISTENING FOR MAIN IDEAS

Read the list of issues. Listen to the TV talk show. Put the issues in order from 1 to 5. (Which issue is discussed first, second, third, and so on.)

_____ The difference between a nanny and a sitter

__1__ Child care in the United States

_____ What a nanny does

_____ What one husband thinks about male nannies

_____ How this man became a nanny

C. LISTENING FOR DETAILS

Listen to the TV talk show again. Circle the letter of the sentence that is true.

1. a. <u>More</u> than 50 percent of families with children in the United States pay for child care.

   b. <u>Fewer</u> than 50 percent of families with children in the United States pay for child care.

2. a. A <u>woman</u> is sometimes called a manny.

   b. A <u>man</u> is sometimes called a manny.

3. a. A male and female nanny do the <u>same</u> things.

   b. A male and female nanny do <u>different</u> things.

4. a. A <u>sitter</u> usually does household chores.

   b. A <u>nanny</u> usually does household chores.

5. a. This male nanny <u>thinks</u> child care is women's work.

   b. This male nanny <u>doesn't think</u> child care is women's work.

6. a. This male nanny <u>went</u> to a special school.

   b. This male nanny <u>didn't go</u> to a special school.

7. a. <u>Most</u> parents like male nannies.

   b. <u>Some</u> parents like male nannies.

8. a. The woman who hired this male nanny <u>was surprised</u>.

   b. The woman who hired this male nanny <u>wasn't surprised</u>.

9. a. At first, the woman's husband <u>didn't like</u> the manny being alone with his wife.

   b. At first, the woman's husband <u>liked</u> the manny being alone with his wife.

10. a. This male nanny <u>has</u> friends who are mannies.

    b. This male nanny <u>doesn't have</u> friends who are mannies.

Now go back to Section 3A on page 83. Were your predictions correct?

D. LISTENING BETWEEN THE LINES

Listen to the excerpts from Listening One. Discuss these questions with a partner.

Excerpt One

Who likes male nannies? Why? Think of three reasons.

Excerpt Two

1. Are male nannies the same as fathers? What are some differences?

2. Think back to when you were a child. Would you have liked a nanny? If yes, would you have liked a male or female nanny? Why?

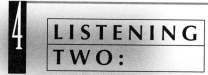

4 LISTENING TWO: Who Is Right for the Job?

A. EXPANDING THE TOPIC

Listen to the conversations. The people are discussing men's and women's work. Who do the people think can do the work? Circle men, women, or both. Then listen again and write the reason.

	WHO CAN DO THE JOB?	REASON
Conversation 1 What does the man think?	men / women / both	
Conversation 2 What does the man think?	men / women / both	
Conversation 3 What does the woman think?	men / women / both	

B. LINKING LISTENINGS ONE AND TWO

Read the information. Then follow the directions.

Statements can be opinions or facts. An opinion is something you believe to be true. Different people can have different opinions about the same thing. You can agree or disagree with an opinion. Facts are statements that are true for everyone.

Look at the sentences. Which are opinions and which are facts? Write an O for opinion and an F for fact. Then compare your answers with those of a partner.

_____ 1. Men can't have babies.

_____ 2. Men can't be male nannies.

_____ 3. Women aren't strong.

_____ 4. Women can't be in the army because it's a man's job.

_____ 5. There are more women in the world than men.

_____ 6. Women take care of children because it's a woman's job.

_____ 7. Men and women can both teach children.

_____ 8. Women can't be mechanics because they can't learn how to fix cars.

What are some other common opinions and facts about men and women? Discuss your ideas with the class.

5 REVIEWING LANGUAGE

A. EXPLORING LANGUAGE: Intonation

In speaking, people use intonation to change the meaning of a word. Intonation is the rising and falling of your voice. The same word with different intonation can have a different meaning.

 ❶ *Listen to the example and discuss the question.*

Example: WOMAN: I've lived in this city for twenty-five years.
          MAN: Really?

Does the man's voice rise or fall? Why?

2 *Listen to the conversations. First, circle the best description of the person's response (a or b). Then in the blanks, write R for rising intonation or F for falling intonation.*

_____ 1. Really.　　　a. The man is surprised.

　　　　　　　　　　b. The man doesn't believe it.

_____ 2. Really.　　　a. The woman is surprised.

　　　　　　　　　　b. The woman doesn't believe it.

_____ 3. Well . . .　　a. The woman wants the man to say more.

　　　　　　　　　　b. The woman is going to say more.

_____ 4. Well . . .　　a. The woman wants the man to say more.

　　　　　　　　　　b. The woman is going to say more.

_____ 5. Hmm . . .　　a. The man is asking a question.

　　　　　　　　　　b. The man is thinking.

_____ 6. Hmm . . .　　a. The man is asking a question.

　　　　　　　　　　b. The man is thinking.

B. WORKING WITH WORDS

1 *Match the words on the left with the definitions on the right.*

_____ 1. agree

_____ 2. disagree

_____ 3. have a problem with

_____ 4. make fun of

_____ 5. strange

_____ 6. there's no difference

_____ 7. typical

a. usual

b. have a different opinion from someone else

c. it's the same thing

d. not normal, very unusual

e. not approve of

f. have the same opinion as someone else

g. tease, laugh at

② *Use the words from Exercise 1 on page 87 to complete the conversation. Then practice the conversation with a partner.*

A: You know, some people think it's not normal to see a male nanny. They think it's a little (1) _____.

B: Yes, I think it's because being a nanny is a (2) _____ job for a woman, not a man.

A: Some people really don't think it's good. They (3) _____ _____ _____ _____ male nannies. They really don't like the idea at all.

B: Well, for me, (4) _____ _____ _____ between male and female nannies. I think they are both good.

A: Sometimes people (5) _____ _____ _____ male nannies. They laugh at them. They think a man is doing a woman's job.

B: Well, I (6) _____. I have a different opinion.

A: I think you and I think the same way about male nannies. We (7) _____!

6 SKILLS FOR EXPRESSION

A. GRAMMAR: Adverbs and Expressions of Frequency

① *Read the sentences. Notice the italicized words. Then answer the questions on page 89.*

◆ A nanny *always* takes care of the children.

◆ A nanny *sometimes* cooks dinner for the children.

◆ A nanny is *usually* a woman.

a. What are the verbs? Circle them.

b. What question do the italicized words answer?

c. In which sentence does the italicized word appear after the verb? What's the verb?

d. In all three sentences, what tense are the verbs in? Why?

FOCUS ON GRAMMAR

See Adverbs and Expressions of Frequency in *Focus on Grammar, Basic.*

Adverbs and Expressions of Frequency

Some adverbs of frequency are:

always	sometimes
usually	rarely
often	never

Some expressions of frequency are:

every (day, week, month)

twice (a week)

three times (a month)

several times (a year)

once in a while

Use adverbs and expressions of frequency to tell how often someone does something.

◆ I **usually** help the children get ready for school.

Adverbs of frequency come after the verb *be.*

◆ A nanny **is usually** a woman.

Adverbs of frequency usually come before other verbs.

◆ A nanny **often lives** with a family.

◆ Husbands **sometimes** worry about male nannies.

Sometimes can also come at the beginning of a sentence.

◆ **Sometimes** husbands worry about male nannies.

Expressions of frequency usually come at the beginning or the end of the sentence.

◆ I pick up the children after school **every day.**

◆ **Once in a while,** we go to the movies.

❷ *Ask six classmates a question beginning, "Do you ever _____?"*
Choose activities from the list below or think of your own activities.
When someone answers "Yes," ask, "How often do you _____?"
The answer must include an expression of frequency. Write the
students' names and their answers.

clean your house   take vacations

dream in English   talk to a good friend

eat dessert   think about someone special

listen to the radio   think about the future

pay bills

Example: STUDENT A: Do you ever clean your house?
             STUDENT B: Yes, I do.
             STUDENT A: How often do you clean your house?
             STUDENT B: I clean my house once a week.

once *a day / a week / a month / a year*

twice *a day / a week / a month / a year*

three times *a day / week / month / year*

every *day / night / week / month / Sunday*

several times *a week*

once in a while

Example: Ming cleans his house once a week.

1. _____.

2. _____.

3. _____.

4. _____.

5. _____.

6. _____.

3 *Interview another student. Ask if men or women in your partner's home culture usually do the things listed in the chart. Write the answers in the chart. Use adverbs of frequency.*

Example: A: Who usually cooks for the family in your home culture, men or women?

B: Men sometimes cook for the family. Women usually cook for the family.

NAME _____ COUNTRY _____	MEN	WOMEN
cook for the family	sometimes	usually
take care of the children		
have jobs outside the home		
repair cars and other things		
manage the money		
are leaders of the country		
are teachers		
are doctors		

Now each student in the class says one thing about his or her partner's home culture. Try to say a different thing from what the student before you says.

Example: Miguel is from Spain. In Spain, men sometimes cook for the family. Women usually cook for the family.

B. STYLE: Asking about and Expressing Opinions

Often in conversation, we want to express opinions on a topic.

Examples:

◆ I **think** women and men should share child care **because** children can learn from both parents.

◆ I **feel** men should take care of the money in a household **because** women do other chores.

Work in groups of four. Take turns choosing an opinion from the list. Read the opinion aloud. The other students either agree or disagree with the opinion. Discuss your opinions and give reasons. Use these words.

I agree.   I disagree / I don't agree.

I really agree.   I don't agree at all.

Opinions

Women are better at some things than men. (Give examples.)

Men are better at some things than women. (Give examples.)

Women should do all the cooking and cleaning in a house.

Women with young children shouldn't work outside the home.

Men should be responsible for all the money in a household.

Men should stay home and take care of children.

A relative, not a child-care worker, should take care of young children.

Example: STUDENT A: Women are better at some things than men.

STUDENT B: I agree. I think women are better at cooking than men because women learn from their mothers.

STUDENT C: I disagree. I feel women are not better at some things than men because . . .

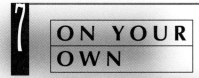

ON YOUR OWN

A. SPEAKING TOPICS: Doing a Class Survey

Step 1: *Look at the list of unusual jobs for men and women. Choose two unusual jobs for men and two unusual jobs for women. Use the jobs from the list or think of your own.*

Unusual Jobs for Men	Unusual Jobs for Women
nanny	truck driver
nurse	mechanic
secretary	electrician
preschool teacher	airplane pilot
midwife	construction worker

Step 2: *Survey students in your class. Find out what they think about men and women doing these jobs and why. Use the questions and responses listed below. Keep track of the different opinions. Then count the total number of responses.*

◆ What do you think about male nannies/female nannies? or

◆ How do you feel about male nannies/female nannies?

◆ I think it's fine. / I have a problem with it. / I think it's strange.
   (I dislike the idea.)   (I really dislike the idea.)

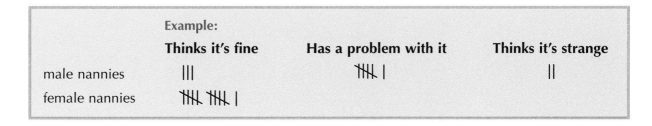

Example:

	Thinks it's fine	Has a problem with it	Thinks it's strange
male nannies	|||	ℍℍ		||
female nannies	ℍℍ ℍℍ			

Step 3: *Discuss the results of your survey with the class. Are you surprised by any of the results? Why or why not?*

B. FIELDWORK

In this unit, you learned about male nannies. Taking care of children is an unusual activity for a man. For the next week, look around in the city or town where you live. Notice the jobs or activities you see men and women doing. Which ones do you think are unusual for a man or a woman? Write down unusual jobs or activities for each and the reason you think it's unusual. Keep a list. Then discuss your findings with the class.

Unusual Jobs/Activities for Men   **Reason I Think It's Unusual**

1. _____   _____

2. _____   _____

3. _____   _____

Unusual Jobs/Activities for Women   **Reason I Think It's Unusual**

1. _____   _____

2. _____   _____

3. _____   _____

Listening Task

Which job or activity do you think is the most unusual for a man?
Which job or activity do you think is the most unusual for a woman?

GOOD-MOOD FOODS

1 APPROACHING THE TOPIC

A. PREDICTING

Look at the picture. Read the title of the unit. Discuss these questions with the class.

1. Name the foods in the picture.

2. How does the man feel? Which foods do you think he should eat? Which foods do you think he shouldn't eat? Why?

3. What do you think the title of the unit means?

B. SHARING INFORMATION

❶ *What do you think about when choosing a meal to eat? Rank the items in the list in order of importance from 1 to 5; 1 is the most important to you and 5 is the least important to you.*

_____ It tastes good.

_____ It's good for you.

_____ It's cheap to buy.

_____ It's easy to make.

_____ Everyone at my house likes it.

❷ *Write a reason for your first and last choices. Then work in a small group. Explain your answers.*

Reason for choice 1: _____

Reason for choice 5: _____

Example:

A: I chose a meal that's cheap to buy because I have a big family.

B: Really? I chose a meal that's easy to make because I'm a bad cook.

2 PREPARING TO LISTEN

A. BACKGROUND

People have different reasons for choosing foods. You may choose a food because it's good for you. The food pyramid on page 97 shows how many servings from each food group you need to stay healthy. People should eat more foods from the groups at the bottom of the pyramid, like fruits and vegetables. They are very good for you because they have a lot of vitamins and minerals. On the other hand, people should eat fewer servings of the foods from the groups at the top of the pyramid because they aren't as good for you.

❶ *Work in pairs. Look at the food groups in the pyramid. Answer the following questions.*

1. What are the names of the different food groups?

2. What food group does each of the following foods belong to?

   bananas   oranges
   beef   turkey
   chili peppers   wheat
   chocolate

3. What are some foods that are good for you? What are some foods that are not good for you?

4. What is one food from each group that you like? What is one food from each group that you don't like?

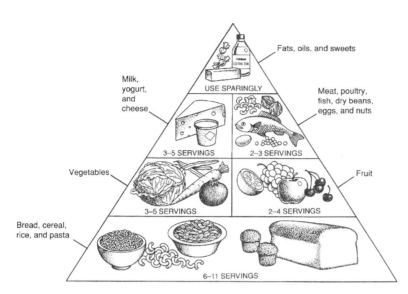

Fats, oils, and sweets

Milk, yogurt, and cheese

USE SPARINGLY

Meat, poultry, fish, dry beans, eggs, and nuts

3–5 SERVINGS   2–3 SERVINGS

Vegetables

Fruit

3–5 SERVINGS   2–4 SERVINGS

Bread, cereal, rice, and pasta

6–11 SERVINGS

❷ *Look at the following foods. What are they made with? Name two ingredients in each one. The first one is done for you. Do you think any of these foods are good for you? Are any of them bad for you?*

1. Banana Muffin

ingredients:

bananas

wheat flour

2. Turkey Sandwich

ingredients:

_____

_____

3. Hamburger

ingredients:

_____

_____

4. Chocolate Chip Cookies

ingredients:

_____

_____

B. VOCABULARY FOR COMPREHENSION

❶ *Read the conversations. The people are talking about their moods, or feelings. Choose the best words to complete the definitions of the underlined words.*

1. A: What are you thinking about?

B: Oh, I'm thinking about my girlfriend. She's so great! I want to be with her all the time.

A: Wow. It sounds like you're <u>in love</u>.

To be <u>in love</u> is to _____.

a. feel love for someone   **b.** love to do something

2. A: What are you doing after work?

B: First, I'm going to the gym to get some exercise. Then I'm going to go out dancing.

A: You're so <u>energetic</u>. Don't you ever get tired?

To be <u>energetic</u> is to be _____.

a. active and full of energy   **b.** busy and tired

3. A: What's the matter? You look <u>miserable</u>.

B: I am. I really miss my family. I feel so unhappy because they live far away and I can't see them.

To be <u>miserable</u> is to be very _____.

a. angry   **b.** sad

4. A: What did you do today?

B: I took care of my friend's three children. They are so active! I was running all day. Now I'm <u>exhausted</u>.

A: You should sit down and rest.

To be <u>exhausted</u> is to be very _____.

a. tired   **b.** active

5. A: Do you want to go to the movies with me?

B: No way! I don't have time to go to the movies!

A: Gee, you sure are <u>irritable</u>.

B: Sorry. I'm having a bad day.

To be <u>irritable</u> is to be _____.

a. easily angered or made unhappy   **b.** busy and unable to have fun

6. A: Kathy is such an <u>upbeat</u> person.

   B: I agree. She's always happy, even when she has problems.
   I wish I could be more like her.

   To be <u>upbeat</u> is to _____.
   a. feel good or happy   b. have problems

7. A: It's almost your turn to give a speech in front of the class.
   How do you feel?

   B: I feel really <u>nervous</u>. I hate speaking in front of people. My
   knees are shaking!

   To be <u>nervous</u> is to be _____.
   a. sad or unhappy   b. worried or afraid

8. A: You gave a great speech. You looked so <u>relaxed</u>. How do you
   stay so calm?

   B: I'm lucky. I like speaking in front of people. I never get
   nervous.

   To be <u>relaxed</u> is to be _____.
   a. lucky   b. calm; not nervous

9. A: What's wrong? You look worried about something.

   B: Yes, I'm really <u>stressed</u> right now. I have a lot of work to do,
   and my mother is sick.

   A: I'm sorry to hear that.

   To be <u>stressed</u> is to _____.
   a. be worried or pressured   b. have a lot to do because of
                                    problems in life

❷ *All of the words in Exercise 1 describe moods. Some are good moods
and some are bad moods. Make a list of good and bad moods on a
separate piece of paper. Then write a sentence that explains when you
might be in each mood. Compare your list with a partner's.*

Example

Bad Moods: irritable
   ◆ I feel irritable when I'm hungry.

Good Moods: relaxed
   ◆ I feel relaxed after I take a nap.

3 LISTENING ONE: Would You Like to Be on the Radio?

A. INTRODUCING THE TOPIC

You will hear a radio talk show. Listen to these excerpts from the show. Read the questions and discuss the answers with the class.

1. Where are the people?

2. What are the people doing?

3. How do the people feel?

4. What do you think the people will talk about?

B. LISTENING FOR MAIN IDEAS

Marty Moore is a radio talk show host on Street Talk. *He talks to four people on the street. Listen to the conversations. Then read the sentences. Write* **T** *for the sentences that are true and* **F** *for the sentences that are false.*

_____ 1. Some doctors think that foods can change your moods.

_____ 2. Larry wants to be on the radio.

_____ 3. Jenny is hungry.

_____ 4. The food can make Dan feel better.

_____ 5. Barbara wants to try the food that Marty offers.

C. LISTENING FOR DETAILS

Listen again to Marty talking to four different people. Look at the chart and answer the questions.

1. How does each person feel now? Check (✓) the correct mood for each person.

2. What foods can help the people feel better? Check (✓) the foods that Marty tells each person to eat. You may check more than one food.

3. How can the foods make the people feel? Check (✓) the moods for each food. You may check more than one mood for each food.

	HOW DOES THE PERSON FEEL NOW?	WHAT FOOD(S) CAN HELP THE PERSON FEEL BETTER?	HOW CAN THE FOOD(S) HELP THE PERSON FEEL?			
			Energetic	**In Love**	**Relaxed**	**Upbeat**
1. Larry	excited ____ nervous ____	chili peppers —— chocolate ____				
2. Jenny	exhausted ____ relaxed ____	beef ____ bananas ____ bread ____				
3. Dan	miserable ____ stressed ____	chocolate ____ nuts ____ wheat flour ____				
4. Barbara	stressed ____ exhausted ____	turkey ____ beef ____ orange juice ——				

Now go back to Section 3A on page 100. Were your predictions correct?

D. LISTENING BETWEEN THE LINES

Listen to the excerpts from Listening One. Then discuss these questions with the class.

Excerpt One

1. How does the soup smell? How does it taste?

2. Is the man surprised when he tastes it? Why or why not?

Excerpt Two

1. Does the woman want to eat the food? Why or why not?

2. Is she polite to Marty? Why do you think so?

4 LISTENING TWO: What's the Matter?

A. EXPANDING THE TOPIC

1 *Listen to three people who are in bad moods. How do they feel? Why do they feel that way? Write your answers in the chart below.*

	PERSON 1	PERSON 2	PERSON 3
How does the person feel?			
Why does he/she feel that way?			

2 *Work with a partner. Decide what food(s) you think each person should eat to feel better. Then discuss your answers with the class.*

B. LINKING LISTENINGS ONE AND TWO

Work in pairs. Discuss these questions with the class.

1. Do you think foods can change your moods?

2. Do you ever eat foods to change your moods? If so, which foods do you eat?

3. What other things do you do to change your moods? For example, what do you usually do to feel relaxed, upbeat, or energetic?

5 REVIEWING LANGUAGE

A. EXPLORING LANGUAGE

There are three ways to pronounce the plural -*s*.

1. The plural is pronounced /s/ after the voiceless sounds /p/, /t/, /k/, /f/, and /θ/.

2. The plural is pronounced /z/ after vowel sounds and voiced consonant sounds such as /n/ and /r/.

3. The plural is pronounced /ɪz/ after the sounds /s/, /z/, /ʒ/, /tʃ/, and /ʃ/.

❶ *Listen to the three plural endings. Look at the words in the chart below.*

❷ *Look at the words below. Write each word under the correct plural sound on the chart. Then listen and check your answers. Finally, practice saying each word.*

apples	chips	fats	sandwiches
chili peppers	dishes	hamburgers	sweets

s = /s/	s = /z/	s = /ɪz/
carrots	bananas	oranges

B. WORKING WITH WORDS

1 *Work with a partner. Each of the words and phrases goes with one of the verbs in the chart. Some words and phrases can go with more than one verb. Complete the chart. Then think of two more words to add to each column.*

alone	chili peppers	hungry
angry	crazy	in a bad mood
awake	delicious	in a good mood
bad	good for you	in a hurry
beef	hot	stressed

Be	Feel	Look	Made with	Smell	Taste
hot	hot	hot			hot

2 *Discuss the words with your class. Which words describe foods? Which words describe moods?*

3 *Using the questions below, interview a classmate. Share his or her answers with the class.*

1. Are you in a good mood or a bad mood today? Why?

2. How often are you in a hurry to get to school or work?

3. When do you feel angry? What do you do when you feel angry?

4. Look at one of your classmates. How does he/she look today?

5. What's your favorite food? What's it made with?

6. What's one food that smells good? What's one food that smells bad?

7. What's one food that tastes good? What's one food that tastes bad?

SKILLS FOR EXPRESSION

A. GRAMMAR: Count and Non-count Nouns

1 *Read the sentences. Notice the italicized words. Then answer the questions.*

- ◆ *Bananas* help you feel energetic.
- ◆ Have *some soup*.

a. Is the word *bananas* singular or plural? Can you count bananas?

b. Is the word *soup* singular or plural? Can you count soup? What word comes before *soup* in the sentence?

FOCUS ON GRAMMAR

See Count and Non-count Nouns in *Focus on Grammar, Basic.*

Count and Non-count Nouns

Count nouns are the names of people, places, and things. Use ***a, an,*** or ***one*** before a singular count noun. To form the plural of a count noun, add **-s** or **-es**. You may use numbers with count nouns.

- ◆ I ate **a sandwich, an orange,** and **one banana**.
- ◆ He ate **two sandwiches, three oranges,** and **five bananas.**

Some nouns cannot be counted. They are called ***non-count nouns***. Do not put ***a, an,*** or a number before a non-count noun. Do not add **-s** or **-es** to a non-count noun because non-count nouns do not have a plural form. Use a quantity word to indicate the amount of a non-count noun.

- ◆ Try **a glass of orange juice**.
- ◆ We need **a pound of beef**.

Use ***some*** with plural count nouns and non-count nouns in affirmative statements.

- ◆ I bought **some** muffins.
- ◆ Have **some** turkey.

Use ***any*** with plural count nouns and non-count nouns in questions and negative statements.

- ◆ Do we have **any** vegetables?
- ◆ No, we don't have **any** vegetables.

2 *Work in pairs. Play a game of Tic-Tac-Toe.*

To play, Student A and Student B take turns naming the foods in the squares. If the food is a singular count noun, say "a" or "an" before it. If the food is a plural count noun or non-count noun, say "some." If you name a food correctly, put a marker on top of it. The first student to name three foods in a row correctly wins. Then change roles and play again.

	Shopping List
○	rice
	~~chili peppers~~
	flour
	bananas
	milk
○	~~coffee~~
	~~apples~~
	bread
	~~sugar~~
	~~carrots~~
	orange juice
○	~~soup~~

3 *Work in pairs. Take turns asking about the food on the shopping list. Use the question and answers below.*

Do we need any . . . ?   Yes, we need . . .

                                            No, we don't need any . . .

Example: A: Do we need any rice?

                  B: Yes, we need some rice. Do we need any chili peppers?

                  A: No, we don't need any chili peppers.

B. STYLE: Politely Expressing Wants

When ordering food in a restaurant, or when eating at home, it's polite to use *would like* and *will have* to express wants.

Asking about Wants	**Expressing Wants**
◆ What **would** you **like?**	◆ **I'd like** a turkey sandwich, please.
◆ **Would** you **like** anything to drink?	◆ **I'll have** a cup of coffee, please.
◆ **Would** you **like** anything else?	◆ Yes, please. **I'll have** a glass of water.
	Refusing
	◆ No, thank you.
	◆ No, that'll be all, thanks.
	◆ Just the check, please.

1 *Put the conversation in the correct order. Number the lines from 1 to 6. The first one is done for you.*

Waiter/Waitress	**Customer**
_____ Would you like anything to drink with that?	_____ No, that'll be all, thanks.
_____ Would you like anything else?	_____ Yes, I'd like a hamburger and some french fries.
__1__ Good evening, are you ready to order?	_____ Yes, please. I'll have some iced tea.

② *Work in pairs.*

Student A: You are a customer in a restaurant. Look at the menu below. Order a meal.

Student B: You are a waiter or waitress. Take your partner's order.

Then change roles. Practice the conversation and then perform it for the class. The class listens and writes down the customer's order.

MARTY'S DINER
MENU

Appetizers

Soup $3.75

Salad......................$5.50

Chips and Salsa $3.00

Beverages

Iced Tea $1.00

Coffee ....$ .85

Milk $1.00

Soda ....$ .80

Orange Juice $1.50

Entrees

Roast Turkey with Mashed Potatoes...............................$9.95

Hamburger with French Fries...$6.99

Spaghetti with Meatballs..$7.00

Grilled Cheese Sandwich...$4.95

Desserts

Chocolate Cake $3.75

Banana Cream Pie.......$3.50

Good Food ◉ Good Prices ◉ Good Service

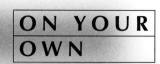

ON YOUR OWN

A. SPEAKING TOPICS: Planning a Potluck Party

1 *A potluck is a party where each guest brings a different dish to eat. Work in a small group to plan a potluck party. Each student chooses a different dish to bring to the party. Make sure your group has at least one appetizer, one main dish, and one dessert. Take turns asking and answering the questions below and write your answers in the chart.*

a. Would you like to bring an appetizer, a main dish, or a dessert?

b. What dish would you like to bring?

c. Why do you like it?

d. What are the main ingredients?

	DISH	WHY YOU LIKE IT	MAIN INGREDIENTS
Appetizer(s)			
Main Dish(es)			
Dessert(s)			

❷ *Each group reports to the class about the dishes they will bring. The class answers these questions:*

    a. Which dishes do you think will taste good?

    b. Which dishes are good for you?

    c. Which dishes are good for your moods?

B. FIELDWORK

Work with another student or in a small group. Choose a restaurant where you would like to eat. Go to the restaurant for a meal. Then answer the following questions about the restaurant.

◆ What's the name of the restaurant? _____

◆ Where is it? _____

◆ What did you eat and drink? _____

◆ How did the food look, smell, and taste? _____

◆ How did the restaurant look? _____

◆ Was the waiter or waitress polite? _____

◆ How did you feel after your meal? _____

Report back to your class with a review of the restaurant. Would you recommend the restaurant to your classmates?

Listening Task

Listen to your classmates' presentations. Which restaurant(s) do you want to go to? Why? Which restaurant(s) don't you want to go to? Why not?

AN ICE PLACE TO STAY

1 APPROACHING THE TOPIC

A. PREDICTING

Look at the photograph. Read the title of the unit. Discuss these questions with the class.

1. Where do you think this picture was taken?

2. What is the man doing there?

3. What is the man wearing? What time of year do you think it is?

4. What do you think the title of the unit means? What kind of place does it describe?

111

B. SHARING INFORMATION

❶ *Look at the list. Rank the things you think about when choosing a place to visit. Mark each item Very Important (VI), Somewhat Important (SI), or Not Important (NI).*

_____ weather (what the weather's like)

_____ location (how far it is from home)

_____ language (what language the people speak)

_____ cost (how expensive it is to visit)

_____ activities (things to do there)

_____ sights (places to see there)

_____ lodging (places to stay there)

_____ people (friends and family to visit)

❷ *Now compare your answers in a group. Tell why each item is very important, somewhat important, or not important to you.*

❸ *In your group, discuss this question:*

Where can you get information to plan a vacation?

2 PREPARING TO LISTEN

A. BACKGROUND

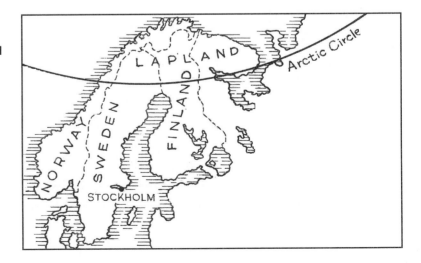

Sweden is a very large country in northern Europe. It covers 977 miles from north to south. Every year tourists come from all over the world to visit Sweden's cities, see the interesting sights, and enjoy the outdoors. It's easy to find nature in Sweden. Fifty percent of Sweden is forest, or covered in trees, and many wild animals live there. There are 96,000 lakes in Sweden and in the north there is a long range of tall mountains.

Tourists planning a trip to Sweden must think about the weather when choosing the best time to visit. In summer, the days are long and warm. The sun shines almost all day and night, and in the north, visitors can see the midnight sun. Winter, on the other hand, is cold and dark. Sometimes there are only a few hours of sunlight each day.

Tourists must also think about costs when planning a trip to Sweden. Shops, restaurants, and lodging are all very expensive. So if you're on a budget, you'll need to watch your money in Sweden.

Work in a small group. Look at the map on page 112. Discuss your answers to the questions.

1. Where is Sweden? What's the weather like? What do you know about Sweden?

2. What activities do you think you can do there in the summer? What activities do you think you can do there in the winter?

3. What time of year do you think tourists usually visit Sweden? Why do you think so?

4. Have you ever visited Sweden? If not, would you like to visit Sweden? Why or why not?

B. VOCABULARY FOR COMPREHENSION

❶ *Read the paragraphs. Notice the underlined words. If you don't know a word, look it up in the dictionary. Then discuss the meanings of the words with the class.*

Tourists planning a trip to Sweden have many different kinds of vacations to choose from. People who prefer big cities may choose to visit Stockholm, Sweden's largest city. In Stockholm, tourists can go shopping, visit <u>museums</u> to learn about the local history and culture, and go to <u>art galleries</u> to see some Swedish art. In and around Stockholm there are also some beautiful old <u>churches</u> and castles to visit. In the evening, tourists can eat out in restaurants and visit the local <u>bars</u> to have a drink.

Tourists who enjoy nature can find many outdoor activities to do in Sweden. In the summer months, you can go swimming or hiking or just relax on the beach. Those who enjoy cold-weather activities, such as skiing and ice-skating, can visit Sweden in the winter, when there is always a lot of snow and ice on the ground.

There are also many different kinds of <u>lodging</u>, or places to stay, in Sweden. Travelers can stay at large <u>hotels</u> or they can choose to be <u>guests</u> at small country <u>inns</u>, where they may be treated to a home-cooked breakfast. Budget travelers may prefer to stay at a youth hostel, where they can share a room for very little money. Those who really want to save money and enjoy nature can stay at <u>campsites</u> and sleep outdoors under the trees in a <u>sleeping bag</u>.

❷ *Look at the pictures. Look at the words below. Write the number of the picture next to the correct word.*

Picture 1   Picture 2   Picture 3

Picture 4   Picture 5   Picture 6

_____ cross-country   _____ dogsledding   _____ ice fishing
       skiing   _____ snowmobiling   _____ snowshoeing
_____ sauna

❸ *Cross out the word in each row that does* not *belong. Then compare your answers with a partner. Explain why you think each word doesn't belong.*

1.	church	art gallery	museum	lodging
2.	inn	sleeping bag	hotel	campsite
3.	dogsledding	sauna	snowshoeing	ice fishing
4.	guest	tourist	traveler	bar

3 LISTENING ONE: An Unusual Vacation

A. INTRODUCING THE TOPIC

You will hear about travel in Sweden. Listen to the beginning of "An Unusual Vacation." Circle the answer to each question.

1. What are you listening to?
   a. a TV commercial
   b. a telephone recording
   c. a radio show

2. What is it about?
   a. travel information about Sweden
   b. airplane flights to Sweden
   c. winter activities in Sweden

3. What will you hear more about?
   a. campsites in Sweden
   b. large hotels in Sweden
   c. a special winter hotel in Sweden

4. What do you think the listening will tell you? Circle more than one answer.
   a. the name of the hotel
   b. the location of the hotel
   c. the cost of the hotel
   d. how to get to the hotel
   e. things to do at the hotel
   f. things to do near the hotel

B. LISTENING FOR MAIN IDEAS

*Read the sentences. Listen again. Write **T** for the sentences that are true and **F** for the sentences that are false.*

_____ 1. The Ice Hotel is open all year long.

_____ 2. The Ice Hotel is made from ice and snow.

_____ 3. The Ice Hotel is a cheap place to stay.

_____ 4. There are only guest rooms at the Ice Hotel.

_____ 5. The rooms are warm at night.

_____ 6. There are many activities to do near the Ice Hotel.

C. LISTENING FOR DETAILS

Listen again. Check (✓) the things you can find in the Ice Hotel and the things you can see or do near the Ice Hotel.

Things <u>in</u> the Ice Hotel		**Things <u>near</u> the Ice Hotel**	
1. guest rooms	_____	1. a sauna	_____
2. a bar	_____	2. cross-country skiing	_____
3. a restaurant	_____	3. snowshoeing	_____
4. an art gallery	_____	4. a museum	_____
5. a church	_____	5. dogsledding	_____
6. beds	_____	6. snowmobiling	_____
7. doors	_____	7. a shopping center	_____
8. a bathroom	_____	8. ice fishing	_____
9. closets	_____	9. a new church	_____
10. sleeping bags	_____	10. a restaurant	_____

Now go back to Section 3A on page 115. Were your predictions correct?

D. LISTENING BETWEEN THE LINES

Listen to the excerpts from Listening One. Discuss the questions in class.

Excerpt One

1. Where is the Ice Hotel located? How cold does it get there in the winter? How short can the days get in the winter?

2. What kind of travelers choose to visit Sweden in the winter? Why do you think they want to visit in the winter?

3. Would you like to visit in the winter? Why or why not?

Excerpt Two

1. Why do you think some people want to get married at the Ice Hotel?

2. What do you think it's like staying at the Ice Hotel? Why do you think people want to stay there?

3. Would you like to stay at the Ice Hotel? Why or why not?

4 LISTENING TWO: Vacations around the World

A. EXPANDING THE TOPIC

One way to get information to plan a vacation is to read travel brochures. You can get travel brochures about many different places from a travel office.

1. *Look at the different travel brochures. What place does each brochure describe? What do you know about these places?*

2. *Listen to the information about three different vacations. Write the number of the vacation under the correct brochure.*

3. *Listen again. Write the activities, lodging, and time of year to travel for each vacation.*

Brochure A	Brochure B	Brochure C

Himalayan Mountain Adventure
Do you love nature and beautiful scenery? Do you enjoy hiking and camping? Then this is the trip for you!

Activities:

go _____

enjoy _____

meet _____

Lodging: _____

Time of Year: _____

Southern California Vacation
This travel package will take you to Hollywood and Disneyland, the happiest place on Earth!

Activities:

visit _____

take a tour of _____

go _____

visit _____

Lodging: _____

Time of Year: _____

Balinese Cultural Holiday
Travel to the Indonesian island of Bali for a relaxing and educational vacation.

Activities:

relax _____

study _____

learn how to _____

Lodging: _____

Time of Year: _____

B. LINKING LISTENINGS ONE AND TWO

*You have heard about some different places to take a vacation. Read the questions and write **A, B, C,** or **D**. Then compare your answers in a group. Explain your answers.*

A = The Ice Hotel   C = Southern California
B = The Himalayan Mountains   D = Bali, Indonesia

____ 1. Which place do you think is best for weather?

____ 2. Which place do you think is best for lodging?

____ 3. Which place do you think is best for indoor activities?

____ 4. Which place do you think is best for outdoor activities?

____ 5. Which place do you think is best for sights to see?

____ 6. Which place do you think is the cheapest to visit?

____ 7. Which place do you think is the most expensive?

____ 8. Which place would you like to visit?

5 REVIEWING LANGUAGE

A. EXPLORING LANGUAGE: Word Stress with *Can* and *Can't*

In affirmative statements and questions, the word *can* is not stressed. It sounds like /kən/. In negative statements, the word *can't* receives stress. It is longer or louder than other words.

Listen to these examples.

AFFIRMATIVE STATEMENT: You can ski near the Ice Hotel.
QUESTION: Can you shop?
NEGATIVE STATEMENT: No, you can't shop.

1 *Listen to these sentences. Check (✓) the correct column. Is the sentence affirmative (**can**) or negative (**can't**)?*

	Affirmative	Negative
1.		
2.		
3.		
4.		
5.		
6.		

2 *Listen again. Write the sentences on the lines. Then say them out loud. Underline the stressed words.*

1. _____

2. _____

3. _____

4. _____

5. _____

6. _____

3 *Work in pairs. Take turns reading the sentences from Exercise 2. Stress **can't** by saying it louder or longer. Do not stress **can**. Explain why each sentence is true or false according to what you heard in Listening One.*

B. WORKING WITH WORDS

❶ *Match the phrases on the left with the definitions on the right.*

_____ 1. be adventurous

_____ 2. go cross-country skiing

_____ 3. go hiking

_____ 4. go to amusement parks

_____ 5. have fun

_____ 6. look at the scenery

_____ 7. relax on the beach

_____ 8. stay at youth hostels

_____ 9. take a sauna

_____10. take a tour

a. enjoy yourself

b. go to parks where you can go on rides, play games, and see shows

c. lie on the beach and rest

d. look at the outdoor surroundings or view

e. stay at inexpensive lodging, usually for young travelers

f. visit a place or places, usually with a tour guide

g. try new and unusual things

h. go skiing over the countryside

i. take a long walk outdoors, usually in nature

j. sit in a room filled with hot air or steam

❷ *Now use the words and phrases from Exercise 1 to complete the following lists. When you are finished, compare your answers with the class. Then think of two more activities to add to each list.*

Indoor Activities	Outdoor Activities	Indoor or Outdoor Activities

❸ *Work in pairs. Take turns saying whether you like or don't like to do the activities from Exercise 2. Explain your answers.*

6 SKILLS FOR EXPRESSION

A. GRAMMAR: Modal Verbs *Can* and *Can't*

1 *Read the sentences. Notice the italicized words. Then answer the questions.*

What *can* you *do* at the Ice Hotel?

You *can have* a drink at the bar.

You *can't go* swimming.

a. What are the verbs in each sentence? What form is the main verb?

b. What does *can* mean? What does *can't* mean?

Can and Can't

FOCUS ON GRAMMAR

See *Can* and *Can't* for Ability and Possibility in *Focus on Grammar, Basic.*

Use *can* to talk about ability, things you are able to do. Use *can't* to talk about inability.	I **can** ice skate. I took lessons last year. My brother **can't** ski. He's never tried it.
Use *can* to talk about possibility, things that are possible. Use *can't* to talk about things that are not possible.	You **can** stay at the Ice Hotel in the winter when the weather is cold. You **can't** stay at the Ice Hotel in the summer because the hotel turns into water every summer.
Can and *can't* come before the main verb. The main verb is in the base form.	You **can go** ice fishing in Sweden. You **can't go** ice fishing in Brazil.
Use *can* and *can't* in questions and short answers. Do not use a main verb in a short answer.	**Can** you swim? Yes, I **can.** **Can** Ellen snowshoe? No, she **can't.**

2 *Write five yes/no questions to find out your classmates' abilities. Interview two classmates.*

Example: A: Can you dance?

B: Yes, I can.

A: Can you ice skate?

B: No, I can't.

Write your classmates' names and answers on a separate piece of paper.

Example:	**Miguel**	**Hiroshi**
Can you dance?	yes	yes
Can you ice skate?	no	yes

When you're finished, report to your class. Pay attention to your pronunciation of **can** *and* **can't.**

Example: Miguel can dance and Hiroshi can dance, too. Miguel can't ice skate, but Hiroshi can.

3 *Work in pairs. Student A makes a statement telling if an activity is possible or not possible* **at** *or* **near** *the Ice Hotel. Student B agrees or disagrees. Then change roles.*

Examples:

go cross-country skiing	A: You can go cross-country skiing near the Ice Hotel.
	B: That's right.
have dinner	B: You can have dinner at the Ice Hotel.
	A: No, you can't! There is no restaurant at the Ice Hotel.

a. take a shower

b. visit an art gallery

c. go dogsledding

d. go shopping

e. go to church

f. have a drink

g. play tennis

h. go swimming

i. get married

j. take a sauna

B. STYLE: Making Polite Requests

Can is also used to make polite requests, to politely ask for something. *Could* and *would* are modal verbs that are also used in polite requests. Use *please* to make your request even more polite. When you include a question word in your request, always put the verb at the end of the sentence.

1 *Look at the chart. Notice the ways to request information, answer politely, say "Thank you," and say "You're welcome."*

Requesting Information

* Excuse me. **Can** you **please** tell me **where** the rest room **is?**
* **Could** you tell me the hours of the post office, **please?**
* **Would** you **please** tell me the cost of an airplane ticket to New York?

- -

Answering Politely

* Certainly. It's on the first floor.
* Sure, it's open from 8:00 to 5:00.
* Sorry, I don't know.

- -

Saying "Thank You"

* Thank you.
* Thanks a lot.
* Well, thanks anyway.

- -

Saying "You're Welcome"

* Don't mention it.
* No problem.
* You're welcome.

② *Work with a partner. Student A looks at the exercise. Student B looks at Student Activities, page 160.*

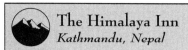

The Himalaya Inn
Kathmandu, Nepal

Tourist Information

Local Restaurants

The Hungry Eye
Kind of food: Indian
Location: across the street
Cost of a meal: about two dollars

Fuji Restuarant
Kind of food: Japanese
Location: near the Royal Palace
Cost of a meal: about eight dollars

Post Office
Hours: Sunday–Friday, 8 A.M. to 7 P.M.
       Saturday, 11 A.M. to 3 P.M.

Bank
Hours: Sunday–Thursday, 10 A.M. to 2 P.M.
       Friday, 10 A.M. to noon

The Royal Palace
Hours: 10:30 A.M. to 4 P.M. daily
Cost to enter: about twenty cents

Student A: You are a clerk at the information desk of the Himalaya Inn in Kathmandu, Nepal. Look at your list of information and answer your partner's requests.

Now change roles.

Student A: You are a guest staying at the Sunset Hotel in Los Angeles, California. Ask your partner polite questions to get the following information. Write your answers below. If you don't know how to spell a word, ask your partner to spell it for you.

1. The location of the Hard Rock Cafe: _____

2. The cost of a meal at the Dining Room restaurant: _____

3. The telephone number of the tourist office: _____

4. The hours of Disneyland on Friday: _____

5. The cost of a ticket to Disneyland for children: _____

6. The hours of Universal Movie Studios: _____

ON YOUR OWN

A. SPEAKING TOPICS: Role Play

Work with a partner. Do the following role play exercise.

1. Choose a vacation place to talk about. It can be a city or country you lived in or visited. Fill in information about your place in the chart on page 125. You'll need to write about the weather, best time of year to visit, activities to do there, sights to see, and lodging.

2. Now work with a partner. You are going to ask for information about your partner's vacation place and then your partner will ask you questions about your place. First, find out the name of your partner's place. Then write questions in the chart to ask your partner. See the example. Use **can, could,** and **would** in your questions.

TOPICS	YOUR PLACE	QUESTIONS	YOUR PARTNER'S PLACE
Weather		Could you tell me about the weather in _____?	
Best time of year to visit			
Activities			
Sights to see			
Lodging			

3. Now do the role play with your partner.

Student A: You want to travel to your partner's place. Ask the questions in the chart.
Student B: You are a travel agent. Answer your partner's questions.

Begin like this:

A: "Could you give me some information about _____?"

B: "Sure. What would you like to know?"

4. When you are finished, change roles.

5. Practice one of your conversations for the class.

Listening Task

Listen to your classmates' role plays and write the following information.

Which place would you like to visit? _____

Name of the place: _____

Two activities you can do there: _____

Two sights you can see there: _____

B. FIELDWORK

❶ *Work in pairs. Think of a country or a city that you would like to visit. Go to a travel agency and interview a travel agent or call the travel bureau for the country. Ask questions to get information about the topics listed below. If you can, get some travel brochures about the place. Or look on the Internet for the information.*

Country or city: _____

Weather: _____

Best time of year to visit: _____

Activities: _____

Sights to see: _____

Lodging: _____

Cost: _____

❷ *Tell the class about the place you want to visit. Show them any brochures or pictures you have.*

Listening Task

Listen to your classmates' presentations and answer these questions:

Which place sounds most interesting? _____

Why? _____

STAYING HEALTHY

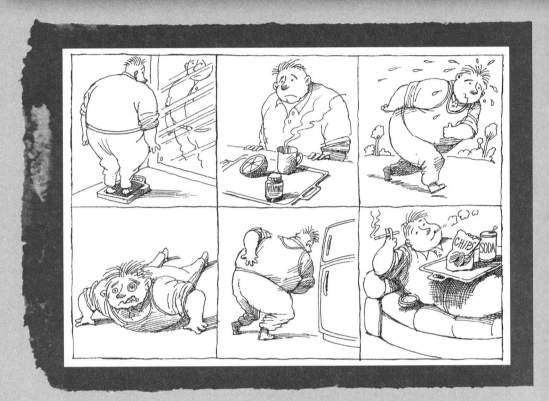

1 APPROACHING THE TOPIC

A. PREDICTING

Look at the cartoon. Read the title of the unit. Discuss these questions with the class.

1. What is the man doing in each picture? How does he feel?

2. Do you ever do any of these activities?

3 Do you think the man is healthy or unhealthy? Why?

4. Look at the title of the unit. What do you think the unit will be about?

B. SHARING INFORMATION

❶ *Work in a small group. Make a list of activities that are good for your health and a list of activities that are bad for your health. The first two are done for you.*

Healthy Activities	Unhealthy Activities
exercise	smoking
_____	_____
_____	_____
_____	_____
_____	_____
_____	_____

❷ *Look at the lists you made in Exercise 1. Discuss these questions in your group.*

1. Which of these activities do you do? How often?

2. Which activity do you think is the best for your health? Why?

3. Which activity is the worst for your health? Why?

PREPARING TO LISTEN

A. BACKGROUND

One way to stay healthy is to eat healthy food, exercise, and watch your weight. But these days many people are overweight; they are too heavy. In fact, up to 70 percent of Americans are overweight. So a lot of people want to lose weight.

One way that people try to lose weight is by going on a diet. When you go on a diet, you eat fewer calories. You can eat less food or eat food that is low in calories. Another way to lose weight is to exercise more. Some people also try using weight-loss remedies. Weight-loss remedies are diet pills or drinks that people use to lose weight. Some people even go to a doctor who can do surgery to take fat off their bodies.

Look at the different ways to lose weight. Read the questions and write **yes, usually, no,** *or* **I don't know** *in the chart. Then compare your answers with a partner. Which is the best way to lose weight? Which is the worst way?*

	GO ON A DIET	EXERCISE MORE	USE WEIGHT-LOSS REMEDIES (Diet Pills or Drinks)	HAVE SURGERY
Health (Is it healthy?)				
Convenience (Is it easy?)				
Cost (Is it inexpensive?)				
Effectiveness (Does it work well?)				
Speed (Is it fast?)				

B. VOCABULARY FOR COMPREHENSION

Read the sentences and guess the meanings of the underlined words. Then match the words with the definitions on page 131.

1. One way to lose weight is to stop eating <u>fattening foods</u> such as cheese, chocolate, or ice cream.

2. I saw a picture of a man who weighs 400 pounds. It's <u>amazing</u> that a person can be that heavy.

3. I'm overweight. I need to go on a diet and <u>lose weight</u>.

4. I think aspirin is the best <u>remedy</u> for a headache. It always makes my headache go away.

5. I have a really bad cold. I feel <u>terrible</u>.

6. My baby has gained a <u>pound</u> since last week. Last week he weighed twelve pounds, and this week he weighs thirteen pounds.

7. One way to <u>prevent</u> health problems is to eat healthy foods, exercise every day, and get enough sleep. Doing those things will help to stop you from getting sick.

8. When I go on a diet I count all the <u>calories</u> I eat. I eat a lot of carrots because they only have a few calories, and I never eat cake or cookies because they have a lot of calories.

9. If you eat too much food and don't exercise enough, you might <u>gain weight</u>. You will get heavier.

10. This medicine stopped my headache, but it gave me a stomachache. The stomachache was a surprising <u>side effect</u>.

11. I like <u>natural</u> fruit juice because it's made with real fruit, not artificial ingredients.

12. I grow <u>herbs</u> such as parsley, mint, and cilantro in my garden. I use them for cooking or for making tea.

____	1. amazing	**a.**	get thinner
____	2. calories	**b.**	get heavier
____	3. fattening foods	**c.**	surprising; unbelievable
____	4. gain weight	**d.**	stop something from happening
____	5. herbs	**e.**	foods that can make you fat
____	6. lose weight	**f.**	a unit of weight equal to 16 ounces, or .454 kilograms
____	7. natural	**g.**	a measure of the energy in food that the body uses
____	8. pound	**h.**	an unexpected result that a medicine has on your body
____	9. prevent	**i.**	coming from nature; not man-made or artificial
____	10. remedy	**j.**	plants used to make medicines or to flavor foods
____	11. side effect	**k.**	something you can do or take to correct a health problem
____	12. terrible	**l.**	very bad

3 LISTENING ONE: Thin-Fast

A. INTRODUCING THE TOPIC

Listen to the man talking about Thin-Fast. Then answer the questions.

1. What are you listening to?

   a. a radio advertisement

   b. a radio news show

   c. a conversation in a doctor's office

2. What is Thin-Fast?

   a. a diet book

   b. a weight-loss remedy

   c. an exercise machine

3. What will the listening be about? Circle more than one answer.

    a. how to use Thin-Fast

    b. how Thin-Fast works

    c. how old it is

    d. where it comes from

    e. what it's made of

    f. what it looks like

    g. how it makes you feel

    h. how it tastes

    i. how much it costs

B. LISTENING FOR MAIN IDEAS

Read the sentences. Then listen to the radio advertisement for Thin-Fast Diet Tea. Circle the best answers to complete each sentence.

1. The woman _____ weight.

    a. lost

    b. gained

2. With Thin-Fast you _____ go on a diet.

    a. have to

    b. don't have to

3. With Thin-Fast you _____ exercise.

    a. have to

    b. don't have to

4. Thin-Fast is _____.

    a. healthy

    b. unhealthy

5. Thin-Fast has _____ ingredients.

    a. man-made

    b. natural

C. LISTENING FOR DETAILS

Read the sentences. Then listen to the radio advertisement again. Write **T** *for the sentences that are true and* **F** *for the sentences that are false.*

_____ 1. Mary Ann lost seventy-five pounds.

_____ 2. You drink Thin-Fast once a day.

_____ 3. Thin-Fast stops you from feeling hungry.

_____ 4. With Thin-Fast you can eat fattening foods and lose weight.

_____ 5. Thin-Fast prevents 100 percent of the fat you eat from turning into fat on your body.

_____ 6. Thin-Fast has some side effects.

_____ 7. The ingredients in Thin-Fast are new.

_____ 8. Thin-Fast makes you feel energetic.

_____ 9. Thin-Fast comes in two different flavors.

_____ 10. You can buy Thin-Fast over the telephone.

Now go back to Section 3A on page 132. Were your predictions correct?

D. LISTENING BETWEEN THE LINES

Listen to three excerpts from Listening One. Discuss these questions.

Excerpt One

1. Why was the woman unhappy before? Why is she happy now?

2. Did the woman want to lose weight for her health? Why or why not?

3. Why do you think most people want to lose weight?

4. Do you think more women than men want to lose weight? Why?

Excerpt Two

1. How does Thin-Fast help you to lose weight?

2. Does the man really believe that Thin-Fast works? Why or why not?

3. Do you think Thin-Fast works? Why or why not?

Excerpt Three

1. Does the woman think Thin-Fast is safe and healthy? Why?

2. Do you think that using Thin-Fast is safe and healthy? Why or why not?

3. How old are the ingredients in Thin-Fast? Why do you think the woman mentions this?

4 LISTENING TWO: Health Problems and Remedies

A. EXPANDING THE TOPIC

 Look at the pictures of the natural remedies. Then listen to the conversations and fill in the information in the blanks below. Compare your answers with those of another student. Listen again.

Peppermint

Garlic

	What Is the Health Problem?	What Remedy Does the Person Suggest?	Does the Person Want to Try It?
Conversation 1	_____	_____	_____
Conversation 2	_____	_____	_____

B. LINKING LISTENINGS ONE AND TWO

Work in a small group. Answer the questions.

1. List the health problems and remedies in Listening One and Listening Two. Discuss what is similar and what is different among the remedies.

2. Do you think natural remedies are better than artificial medicines? Why or why not? Do you use any natural remedies?

3. Who do you usually ask for health advice? Why?

4. Have you ever used a weight-loss remedy? Did it work?

REVIEWING LANGUAGE

A. EXPLORING LANGUAGE: Sentence Stress

When we speak, we stress some words and not others to make our meaning clear. Stressed words are usually content words (nouns, adjectives, and adverbs). Unstressed words are usually short function or grammar words (prepositions, pronouns, articles, and connecting words).

Listen to these examples:

◆ I was <u>overweight</u> and <u>unhealthy</u>.

◆ I <u>looked terrible</u> and I <u>felt terrible</u>.

◆ I <u>loved</u> to eat <u>fattening foods</u> and I <u>hated exercise</u>.

❶ *Read the following sentences aloud. Underline the words you stress. Compare your sentences with those of a partner.*

1. With Thin-Fast, I lost sixty-five pounds in only three months.

2. You just drink one cup of Thin-Fast twice a day.

3. You don't have to exercise, and you don't have to go on a diet.

4. It's a very safe and healthy way to lose weight.

5. It's made from 100 percent natural herbs.

 ❷ *Now listen to the sentences and practice saying them with a partner.*

B. WORKING WITH WORDS

❶ *Work in pairs. Student A reads sentence A out loud. Student B reads sentence B with a word or phrase from the list. Use the underlined words to help. Student A checks the answers in the Answer Key. Change roles after item 5.*

herbal	side effect
money-back guarantee	take care of yourself
prevent	terrible
product	terrific
remedies	too good to be true

1. A: I have a <u>very bad</u> headache.

   B: You have a _____ headache.

2. A: I make my own tea with <u>herbs</u> from my garden.

   B: You make your own _____ tea.

3. A: I have a book that tells you <u>what to do or take for health problems</u>.

   B: You have a book of health _____.

4. A: Thin-Fast sounds great, but <u>I don't believe it works</u>.

B: Thin-Fast sounds _____.

5. A: I just tried a new medicine that can <u>stop</u> you from getting a cold.

B: It can _____ you from getting a cold.

6. A: I want to buy <u>something to help me lose weight</u>.

B: You want to buy a weight-loss _____.

7. A: I <u>do a lot of healthy things</u>: I eat healthy food, I exercise, and I don't smoke.

B: You really_____.

8. A: I really like my new doctor. He's <u>very good</u>.

B: Your new doctor is _____.

9. A: I just heard about a weight-loss drug that can help you lose weight, but <u>it can also make you sick</u>.

B: The drug has a bad _____.

10. A: If you aren't happy with Thin-Fast, you can <u>return it and get your money back</u>.

B: Thin-Fast has a _____.

❷ *Work in a group. Take turns asking the questions. Everyone in the group answers. Use the words from Exercise 1 in your answers.*

1. Name a food that tastes terrible. Name a food that tastes terrific.

2. Name one herbal remedy. What is it used for?

3. Have you ever seen an ad for a product that was too good to be true? What was the ad for? Why didn't you believe it?

4. What do you think is the best way to prevent a cold?

5. What's one thing you do to take care of yourself?

6. Name a medicine or remedy with a side effect.

7. Have you ever bought something with a money-back guarantee? What did you buy?

6 SKILLS FOR EXPRESSION

A. GRAMMAR: Modal Verbs *Should, Ought to,* and *Have to*

❶ *Read the sentences. Notice the italicized words. Then answer the questions below.*

- ◆ You *should* try Thin-Fast Diet Tea.
- ◆ You *shouldn't* work so hard.
- ◆ You *ought to* take better care of yourself.
- ◆ You *have to* go to a doctor to have surgery.
- ◆ With Thin-Fast, you *don't have to* go on a diet.

a. What are the verbs in each sentence?

b. What form is the main verb in each sentence?

c. What does *should* mean? What does *shouldn't* mean?

d. What does *ought to* mean?

e. What does *have to* mean? What does *don't have to* mean?

Should, Ought to, Have to

FOCUS ON GRAMMAR

See *Should, Ought to,* and *Have to* in *Focus on Grammar, Basic.*

Should, ought to, and ***have to*** are modal verbs. Use *should* and *ought to* to give advice or to talk about what is right to do. Use *shouldn't* to talk about something that is not right to do. Use *have to* or *has to* to talk about something that you must do, something that is necessary. Use *don't have to* or *doesn't have to* to talk about something that is not necessary.

In affirmative and negative statements, ***should, shouldn't,*** and ***ought to*** are followed by the base form of the verb. The modal verb and the main verb stay the same for each person.

◆ **I**		
◆ **You**		
◆ **He**	**should**	
◆ **She**	**ought to**	go on a diet.
◆ **It**	**shouldn't**	
◆ **We**		
◆ **You**		
◆ **They**		

Use ***have to*** and ***don't have to*** with *I, you, we,* and *they.*

◆ **I**	**have to**	see the doctor.
◆ **You**	**don't have to**	go to work when you're sick.

Use ***has to*** and ***doesn't have to*** with *he, she,* or *it.*

◆ **She**	**has to**	take her medicine every day.
◆ **He**	**doesn't have to**	have surgery.

In wh- questions, use ***should*** to ask for advice. ***Ought to*** is rarely used in questions or negatives.

◆ **What**	**should**	I do to lose weight?
◆ **Why**	**should**	he see the doctor?

❷ *Read the conversation. Write the correct modal verbs in the blanks.*

A: Hi. How are you?

B: Oh, not great. I hurt my back yesterday. I'm really in pain.

A: Oh, that's too bad.

B: What do you think I (1) _____ do?

A: Well, you really (2) _____ carry those heavy books.
Maybe you (3) _____ go to bed and rest.

B: That's a good idea, but I (4) _____ go to school
tomorrow to take a test. I can't take it any other day.

A: Then maybe you (5) _____ to see the doctor.

B: No way. I hate going to the doctor.

A: Have you tried any natural remedies? You (6) _____
try Chinese white-flower oil. You (7) _____ go to
the doctor for it.

B: A natural remedy? No thanks.

A: You don't like any of my ideas. Maybe you
(8) _____ ask your other friends for advice!

❸ *Work in a group. Take turns asking what each person should and
shouldn't do for some health problems such as a cold, a backache,
and a stomachache. Write your advice on a separate piece of paper.*

Example: A: What should you do for a cold?
B: I think you should take some aspirin and go to bed.
You shouldn't go to work. How about you? What do
you think?
C: I agree. I also think you should drink hot tea with lemon
and honey. I think you shouldn't go to work either.

Health problems	You should . . .	You shouldn't . . .
a cold	take some aspirin	go to work

B. STYLE: Talking about Problems—Expressing Concern, Giving and Receiving Advice

When someone has a problem, it's polite to express concern and offer some advice.

Expressing Concern

- What's the matter?
- What's wrong?
- That's too bad.
- I'm sorry to hear that.

Giving Advice

- Maybe you should . . .
- Why don't you . . .
- I think you ought to . . .
- Have you tried . . .

Receiving Advice

- That's a good idea.
- Thanks for the advice. I'll give it a try.
- Thanks anyway, but I'd rather . . .

Work with another student. Make up a conversation. Student A has a health problem. Student B expresses concern and gives some advice. Practice the conversation, and then perform it for the class. The other students listen to each conversation and answer these questions.

- What's wrong?
- What's the advice?
- Do you agree with the advice?

7 ON YOUR OWN

A. SPEAKING TOPICS: Preparing a Radio Ad

Products

weight-loss product

baldness remedy

energy pills

product to help you stop smoking

Step 1: *Work with another student. Think of an "amazing" health product, and then write a radio ad. Choose a product from the list on the left, or think of your own. In the ad, one person has a health problem, and the other person gives advice. The "amazing" product solves the health problem. Include the following information:*

♦ What's the name of the product? What does it do? How does it work? How often should you use it? How much does it cost? What's it made of (for example, herbs)?

Step 2: *Practice the ad and then present it to the class. If possible, tape record your ad and give it to your teacher for feedback.*

Listening Task: *Listen to your classmates' presentations. Would you like to try the products?*

B. FIELDWORK

Work in pairs. You will interview three people outside of class about their activities. First write at least five questions about healthy and unhealthy activities. Use the activities from the lists you made in Section 1B on page 128, and think of some more.

Example questions:

♦ How often do you exercise?

♦ Do you smoke?

♦ How often do you eat fattening foods?

As you interview the people, write down the answers. Then report back to the class and discuss these questions:

♦ Do you think more people are healthy or unhealthy?

♦ Who do you think are healthier, men or women?

DO YOU BELIEVE IN IT?

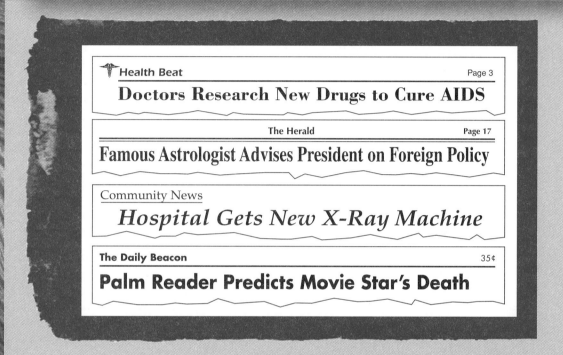

⚕ **Health Beat** — Page 3

Doctors Research New Drugs to Cure AIDS

The Herald — Page 17

Famous Astrologist Advises President on Foreign Policy

Community News

Hospital Gets New X-Ray Machine

The Daily Beacon — 35¢

Palm Reader Predicts Movie Star's Death

1 APPROACHING THE TOPIC

A. PREDICTING

Look at the news headlines. Discuss these questions with the class.

1. What do the doctors want to find? What does <u>research</u> mean?
2. What are X-rays? What kind of information do you get from X-rays?
3. What does <u>predict</u> mean? How is predicting similar to or different from researching something?
4. What does a palm reader do? What kind of information do you get from a palm reader?
5. All of the headlines are about ways to get information. What are the different kinds of information? What do you think about these ways of getting information?

B. SHARING INFORMATION

Palm reading and astrology are two ways to find out about your future. Some people want to know this information. Other people don't want to know. What about you?

Make a list of information you want to know about your future and a list of information you don't want to know. Write your lists on a separate piece of paper. Work in a small group and discuss your lists. Then write lists on the board and do a class survey.

Discuss these questions with the class.

1. What kinds of things did people fifty years ago want to know about their futures? What do you think people fifty years from now will want to know? What are some of the differences?

2. What kinds of things do people in your home culture want to know about the future?

PREPARING TO LISTEN

A. BACKGROUND

Read the paragraphs. Then follow the directions on page 145.

Do you have questions about your health, job, husband, wife, partner, or children? How do you get the information and answers you need?

People have different methods or ways of getting information. Some methods of getting information are scientific. We can get information about our bodies by getting X-rays. X-rays are an example of a scientific method. Scientists know exactly how and why an X-ray works. Other methods are unscientific. This means that the method can't be explained using science. Palm reading is an example of an unscientific method. Some people believe they can get information about their lives by reading the lines in their palms. But just because science can't explain it, does that mean it doesn't work? Many people use unscientific methods and believe that these methods give them the answers they need. They believe these methods work, but they often cannot explain why. When we can't explain why something works or why something happens, we call it an *unexplained phenomenon*.

Look at the pictures. The people in the pictures are dowsers. *They are* dowsing. *Work with a partner. Discuss the questions and write your answers in the first column ("Before You Listen") of the chart below. Then check your answers after you listen to Listening One.*

	BEFORE YOU LISTEN	AFTER YOU LISTEN
1. What information do you think the people in the pictures are trying to find?		
2. Is the method scientific or unscientific?		
3. What do you think people use dowsing for?		
4. How do you think dowsing works?		
5. How old do you think dowsing is?		

B. VOCABULARY FOR COMPREHENSION

❶ *Match the words on the left with the definitions on the right. Look at the pictures on page 145 or use a dictionary to help you.*

_____ 1. divining rod

_____ 2. dowser

_____ 3. dowsing

_____ 4. energy

_____ 5. instrument

_____ 6. location

_____ 7. method

_____ 8. pendulum

_____ 9. shake

_____ 10. swing

_____ 11. underground

a. another word for area

b. below the earth's surface

c. a stick or string with a stone or something heavy on the end that moves from side to side

d. to move up and down or from side to side with fast movements

e. a force or power you cannot see or hear

f. a long stick that dowsers use

g. a person who uses dowsing

h. a way to find something that is lost

i. a way to do something

j. an object used to play music, like a piano or a guitar

k. to move from side to side while hanging

❷ *Work with a partner. Look at the pictures of people dowsing on page 145 and find the following items.*

divining rod

pendulum

dowser

underground water

dowsing

❸ *Which object in the pictures can swing? Which object can shake? Point to them.*

LISTENING ONE: An Introduction to Dowsing

A. INTRODUCING THE TOPIC

Listen to this introduction. Then answer the questions.

1. What are you listening to?

   a. the introduction to a workshop

   b. the introduction to an advertisement

   c. the introduction to a TV show

2. What do you think the woman will talk about? Circle more than one answer.

   a. where dowsing was first found and used

   b. books to read about dowsing

   c. where she is from

   d. people who use dowsing

   e. how to use dowsing every day

   f. the age of dowsing

3. Do you think everyone at this workshop believes dowsing works? Why or why not?

B. LISTENING FOR MAIN IDEAS

Read the sentences. Then listen to the workshop. The sentences are wrong. Cross out the wrong information and correct the sentences.

1. Dowsing is very new.

2. Dowsing can be explained scientifically.

3. Map dowsing is a way to lose things.

4. People use dowsing to ask about important people.

5. The man in the audience believes in dowsing.

C. LISTENING FOR DETAILS

Listen again. Circle the best answer to complete each sentence.

1. The woman thinks everyone at the workshop _____ to dowse.
   a. knows how   **b.** wants to learn   **c.** likes

2. The oldest pictures of dowsing are _____ years old.
   a. 18,000   **b.** 80,000   **c.** 8,000

3. The divining rod _____.
   a. shakes   **b.** swings   **c.** holds water

4. Dowsers believe everything has _____.
   a. a divining rod   **b.** an energy   **c.** a feeling

5. A map dowser holds a _____.
   a. divining rod   **b.** location   **c.** pendulum

6. One woman hired a map dowser to find _____.
   a. water   **b.** an instrument   **c.** a pendulum

7. To get answers with dowsing, you must ask a _____ question.
   a. yes/no   **b.** past   **c.** future

8. The pendulum will _____ one way for "yes" and another way for "no."
   a. shake   **b.** feel   **c.** swing

Now go back to Section 2A on page 145. Were your predictions correct? Write the correct information in the "After You Listen" column.

D. LISTENING BETWEEN THE LINES

Listen to the excerpts from Listening One. Discuss these questions in a small group.

Excerpt One

1. How old is dowsing? Why does the man ask about the age of dowsing?

2. Do you think old methods are better than new methods? Why?

Excerpt Two

1. Why will the man look at a map?

2. Do you think the man believes dowsing works? Why or why not?

3. Do you think something scientific is better than something unscientific? Why?

Excerpt Three

1. What question does the man ask?

2. Why doesn't he let the woman finish?

3. Do you think the woman could get the correct answer? Why or why not?

4 LISTENING TWO: Other Unexplained Phenomena

A. EXPANDING THE TOPIC

Listen to people talking about other unexplained phenomena—things that happen but can't be explained. You will listen two times. Circle the main idea the first time. Then listen again and circle all the details you hear.

	Main Idea	**Details**
Listening 1	Fire walking is . . .	The man says . . .
	1. learning to make fires.	1. his feet didn't burn.
	2. learning about fires.	2. he knows how it works.
	3. learning to walk on fires.	3. fire walking teaches concentration.
		4. the mind is powerful.
Listening 2	Psychokinesis means . . .	The woman says . . .
	1. moving things.	1. *psycho* means "move."
	2. moving things with your mind.	2. a man bent a spoon with his hands.
	3. thinking about moving.	3. a man bent a spoon with his mind.
		4. she knows how it works.

B. LINKING LISTENINGS ONE AND TWO

Many people believe in unexplained phenomena such as fire walking and psychokinesis. They may have seen these events or even done them themselves. Still, many scientists say these things aren't real, and there must be some other explanation or reason for these phenomena.

❶ *Look at each of these unexplained phenomena. Do you believe it works? Write **yes** or **no** and write a possible reason why it works. Then, in a small group, discuss your answers.*

UNEXPLAINED PHENOMENA	DOES IT WORK?	WHY?
Dowsing: Dowsers can find underground water.		
Palm reading: Palm readers can predict your future by looking at your palm.		
Astrology: Astrologists can describe your perfect husband, wife, or partner		
Fire walking: People can walk on fire.		
Psychokinesis: People can move objects with their minds.		

❷ *Discuss these questions with the class.*

1. What other unexplained phenomena do you know about?

2. What could be some explanations for these phenomena?

3. Why do you think some people believe in unexplained phenomena? Why don't other people believe in these things?

REVIEWING LANGUAGE

A. EXPLORING LANGUAGE: Contractions with *Will*

In speaking, we often use contractions. Look at the contractions with *will*. Listen to how they are pronounced.

I will = I'll	it will = it'll
you will = you'll	we will = we'll
he will = he'll	they will = they'll
she will = she'll	

1 *Listen to the questions and answers.*

When will you learn to dowse?	I'll learn how to dowse this weekend.
Where will we learn?	We'll learn at a workshop.
What will he find?	He'll find underground water.
Who will they see?	They'll see a dowser.
What will she teach?	She'll teach dowsing.

2 *Work in pairs. Practice contractions with **will**. Look at the sentences below. Student A reads a question from the list on the left. Student B must find the correct answer from the list on the right and read it out loud. Then switch roles.*

Example:

Student A	**Student B**
What will the weather be like tomorrow?	It'll be sunny.

Student A	**Student B**
What will the weather be like tomorrow?	She'll go home after work.
What time will your mother come home?	It'll be sunny.
Where will people live in fifty years?	They'll live on the moon.
When will the teacher go home?	She'll be home around 8:00.
Where will you live next year?	I'll live here.

B. WORKING WITH WORDS

❶ *Match the words and phrases on the left with the definitions on the right.*

_____ 1. concentration

_____ 2. fire walking

_____ 3. method

_____ 4. psychic ability

_____ 5. powerful

_____ 6. scientific

_____ 7. That's ridiculous.

_____ 8. mind

_____ 9. unexplained phenomenon

a. "That's not believable. It can't be true."

b. the ability to do unusual things with your mind

c. can be explained by science

d. walking on fire

e. very strong

f. a way to do something

g. something that can't be explained using science

h. thinking very hard about only one thing

i. the part of your brain where you think

❷ *Complete the two conversations with the words and phrases from Exercise 1. Then read them out loud with a partner.*

Conversation 1

A: I saw a show on TV last night about people who move things with their minds.

B: They have (**1**) _____ _____. I've heard of that. How do they do it?

A: Well, you know, it's not something science can explain.

B: Yes, I know. It's an (**2**) _____ _____.

A: Yes. I saw a man, Uri Geller . . . he bent a spoon . . . but he didn't touch it.

B: Well, I think our minds are very strong.

A: Yes, I agree. The mind is very (3) _____ .

B: I can't tell you how he did it, but I saw him do it.

A: Science can't explain everything. Many things are not
(4) _____ , but that doesn't mean they aren't real.

B: Right . . .

Conversation 2

A: I read an interesting article in the newspaper.

B: Really, what was it about?

A: Well, you won't believe this. . . . It was about people who walk
on fire.

B: (5) _____ _____ ?

A: Yes, they walk on fire and their feet don't burn.

B: Oh, I can't believe that. It can't be true. (6) _____
_____ !

A: Well, it's true. The teachers say you have to think about one
thing . . . very hard. . . . It's called (7) _____ .

B: So, it's a (8) _____ to teach people concentration.

A: Yes. I saw many people do it. If you think only about walking on
fire, concentrate, and use your (9) _____ , you can learn
to do it.

B: Do you believe that?

A: The article also said not to try this at home! You need to take a
workshop to learn.

B: Don't worry about me. I'm not going to try it!

6 SKILLS FOR EXPRESSION

A. GRAMMAR: Future with *Will*

❶ *Read the following conversation. Then answer the questions that follow.*

A: What will I learn?

B: You'll learn about map dowsing.

A: Will they find my instrument?

B: Yes, they'll find it.

a. What is the tense in each question above? How do you know?

b. Look at each verb after *will* (*'ll*) in the conversation. What is its form?

FOCUS ON GRAMMAR

See Future with *Will* in *Focus on Grammar, Basic.*

Future with *Will*

Use *will* to...	
◆ Talk about general facts about the future ◆ Make predictions about the future	You **will** learn about dowsing. You **will** get a great job. (You**'ll**)
To form statements with *will* ◆ Use *will* plus the base form of the verb	He **will go** to a workshop. (He**'ll**)
To form a negative statement with *will* ◆ Use *will not* or *won't* plus the base form of the verb; notice the contraction	She **will not teach** the workshop. They **won't come** to the workshop.
To form questions ◆ yes/no questions: *will* + subject + base form of the verb ◆ wh- questions begin with a wh-word	**Will we learn** to dowse? **When will** we learn? (When**'ll**)

Workshops are special meetings people go to to learn about something. They can be a few hours or a few weeks long. You usually pay money to attend.

2 *Look at the information about workshops. Use **will** to talk about them. Work in pairs. Student A asks questions about a workshop using the phrases and question words below. Student B finds the information and answers the questions. Ask yes/no and wh- questions. Then switch roles.*

Example: STUDENT A: Where'll I stay for the astrology workshop?

STUDENT B: You'll stay at the Hilton Hotel.

What'll I learn in the _____ workshop?

Who'll teach the _____ workshop?

Where . . . ?

How much . . . ?

When . . . ?

Will I learn about . . . ?

National Workshop Series

Title: Astrology Workshop	**Title:** Palm Reading	**Title:** Fire Walking
Instructor: Anna Woo	**Instructor:** John Bandero	**Instructor:** Jessica Roe
Location: Chicago, Illinois	**Location:** Ontario, Canada	**Location:** Los Angeles, California
Dates: March 7–10	**Dates:** August 15–17	**Dates:** January 1
Accommodations: Hilton Hotel	**Accommodations:** Comfort Inn, $75.00/night	**Accommodations:** No accommodations
Description of Workshop: Learn the basics of astrology: Use a person's birth date to learn about his or her personality and future, and find his or her path in life.	**Description of Workshop:** Learn how to read palms: Understand people's lives by looking at their palms.	**Description of Workshop:** Learn how to use your mind to walk across hot fire. Learn to concentrate and get what you want from strong concentration.
Cost: $395.00	**Cost:** $250.00	**Cost:** $75.00

B. STYLE: Expressing Agreement and Disagreement

❶ *In a conversation, speakers often agree or disagree with each other. Look at the phrases. These are ways to express agreement or disagreement.*

Agree	Not Sure	Disagree
I agree.	I don't know.	I disagree.
Yes, definitely.	I'm not sure.	I don't think so.
I think that's right.	That could be true.	I doubt it.
I think so, too.	It's possible.	That's hard to believe.
Exactly.		That's ridiculous.
		You can't be serious.

❷ *Often in conversation, we make predictions about people and their futures. For example, you might tell a friend, "I think you'll be very successful in the future." You don't know if this is true, but you predict it might be true. Practice making predictions for people in the class. Write five predictions about five different students. Use **will** or **won't** to make a prediction. Then walk around and read the sentences to the students. The students must agree or disagree with each prediction.*

Example:　STUDENT A:　Alicia, you will live in Tokyo next year.

　　　　　　　STUDENT B:　Oh, I don't think so! I won't live in Tokyo! I'll live in Spain!

1. _____

2. _____

3. _____

4. _____

5. _____

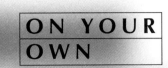

ON YOUR OWN

A. SPEAKING TOPIC: Role Playing

Psychics are people with a special ability to tell you about your past, present, and future—even though they may never have met you before. Some people go to psychics for advice or to learn more about themselves. The power of psychics is another unexplained phenomenon.

Imagine you are a psychic. You have the ability to know the future. Think about the future and what it might be like. What will there be? Will there be life on the moon in ten years? Will everyone have video telephones in five years?

Work in a small group. Look at the list below. You can add other items about the future.

Future Phenomenon	Psychic Prediction
◆ A cure for AIDS	<u>in five years</u>
◆ A female president for the United States	_____
◆ World peace	_____
◆ Video telephones for everyone	_____
◆ Vacations to the moon	_____
◆ _____	_____
◆ _____	_____
◆ _____	_____

Next to each item, make a psychic prediction. When do you think each will happen? In one year? In five years? In ten years? Never? Compare and discuss your predictions in a group. Use the phrases you learned in Section 6B on page 156 to agree or disagree with the other "psychics." Explain your predictions.

Example: STUDENT A: I think there will be cities on the moon in five years.

STUDENT B: I doubt it. I don't think there will be cities on the moon in five years.

STUDENT A: Really? Why not?

STUDENT B: Well, I don't think we will know how to live in space.

B. FIELDWORK

In this unit, you learned about unexplained phenomena. Each culture has its own unexplained phenomena and beliefs.

1. Choose an unexplained phenomenon from your home culture. Look at the list for ideas, or use another one.

2. Use information you know, look in a book, use the Internet, or interview someone about it.

3. Tell the class about the unexplained phenomenon.

Unexplained Phenomena

tea-leaf reading	Ouija boards
numerology	palm reading
feng shui	psychic surgery
tarot-card reading	phrenology

Questions to Guide Your Research

1. Who uses it?

2. How old is it?

3. What do people do? Describe the phenomenon.

4. Where did you learn about it?

5. Do *you* use it? Why or why not?

Listening Task

Listen to your classmates' presentations. Pick one presentation you liked. Try to answer the questions above about the presentation you picked. Did your classmate give enough information for you to answer all the questions?

STUDENT ACTIVITIES

UNIT 1 ◆ OFFBEAT JOBS

5A. EXERCISE 2, page 10

❷ *Student B, listen to Student A say each word, and underline the syllable that is stressed. Check your answers.*

Student B	**Student B**
Listen and underline:	*Say:*
1. salesclerk	6. <u>res</u>taurant
2. difficult	7. in<u>sur</u>ance
3. police	8. <u>taste</u> buds
4. outdoors	9. <u>spi</u>cy
5. unusual	10. ath<u>let</u>ic

UNIT 8 ◆ AN ICE PLACE TO STAY

6B. EXERCISE 2, page 124

② *Student B: You are a guest staying at the Himalaya Inn in Kathmandu, Nepal. Ask your partner polite questions to get the following information. Write your answers. If you don't know how to spell a word, ask your partner to spell it for you.*

1. The location of an Indian restaurant: _____

2. The cost of a meal there: _____

3. The cost of a Japanese meal: _____

4. The hours of the post office on Saturday: _____

5. The hours of the bank on Sunday: _____

6. The cost to enter the Royal Palace: _____

Now change roles.

Student B: You are a clerk at the information desk of the Sunset Hotel in Los Angeles, California. Look at your list of information and answer your partner's requests.

The Sunset Hotel
Los Angeles, California

Tourist Information

Local Restaurants

Hard Rock Cafe
Kind of food: American
Location: in Hollywood
Cost of a meal: about $30

The Dining Room
Kind of food: California style
Location: in Beverly Hills
Cost of a meal: about $50

Local Attractions

Universal Movie Studios
Location: Studio City
Hours: 9 A.M. to 7 P.M. daily
Cost of tour: $33

Disneyland
Summer hours: Sunday–Friday,
9 A.M. to midnight; Saturday, 9 A.M. to 1 A.M.
Cost of ticket: $33 for adults, $25 for children

Tourist Office
Location: 633 5th Street
Telephone: 624-7300

TAPESCRIPT

UNIT 1 ◆ OFFBEAT JOBS

3. LISTENING ONE: What's My Job?

3A. *Introducing the Topic*

Host: Good afternoon everybody, and welcome to *What's My Job?*—the game show about offbeat jobs. I'm Wayne Wonderful and I'm your host. Today's first contestant is Rita, a secretary from Chicago, Illinois.

Rita: Hi, Wayne. I'm so happy to be here! Hi, Mom. Hi, Dad. Hi, Joe. . . .

Host: OK, Rita. Let's get started. You're going to meet some people with unusual jobs. They will describe their jobs. Then you can ask three questions to guess each person's job. You can win 1,000 dollars for each job you guess correctly. Are you ready? Let's welcome our first guest, Peter. OK, Peter, can you tell us a little about your job?

3B. *Listening for Main Ideas*

Host: Good afternoon everybody, and welcome to *What's My Job?*—the game show about offbeat jobs. I'm Wayne Wonderful and I'm your host. Today's first contestant is Rita, a secretary from Chicago, Illinois.

Rita: Hi, Wayne. I'm so happy to be here! Hi, Mom. Hi, Dad. Hi, Joe. . . .

Host: OK, Rita. Let's get started. You're going to meet some people with unusual jobs. They will describe their jobs. Then you can ask three questions to guess each person's job. You can win 1,000 dollars for each job you guess correctly. Are you ready? Let's welcome our first guest, Peter. OK, Peter, can you tell us a little about your job?

Peter: Sure Wayne. At my job, I work with food. My work is very interesting because I can enjoy good food and I can be creative.

Host: That does sound interesting. OK Rita, ask Peter three questions. Then try to guess his job.

Rita: Do you work in a restaurant?

Peter: No, I don't.

Rita: Hmm . . . Do you work in a bakery?

Peter: No, I don't. I work in a factory.

Rita: A factory? Do you make food?

Peter: Yes, I help to make food.

Host: OK. That's three questions. Now Rita, can you guess Peter's job?

Rita: Hmm . . . Are you a chef?

Peter: No, I'm not a chef.

Host: Ah, sorry Rita. So tell us, Peter. What do you do?

Peter: I'm an ice-cream taster.

Rita: An ice-cream taster?

Peter: That's right. I work in an ice-cream factory. I taste the ice cream to make sure that it tastes good. I also think of interesting new flavors to make.

Host: Gee, sounds like a difficult job, Peter. You taste ice cream all day and you get paid for it!

Peter: Yes, that's right. I'm lucky to have such a great job. I really love it!

Host: Good for you. So tell us Peter, is there anything difficult about your job?

Peter: Well . . . I guess so . . . For one thing, I can't eat all the ice cream that I taste. If I ate the ice cream I'd get full. And when I get full, I can't taste the flavors very well. So when I'm at work I don't *eat* all the ice cream. I only taste a little bit of ice cream and then I spit it out. I only eat ice cream when I'm at home, when I can really enjoy it.

Host: I see. That's not so bad. Is there anything else that's difficult?

Peter: Let me think. Well, I have to be very careful to take care of my taste buds. During the week, I don't eat spicy or hot foods.

Host: Really?

Peter: Yes, and I don't drink alcohol or coffee.

Host: Is that so?

Peter: Yes, and I don't smoke either. If I do those things I might hurt my taste buds, and then I wouldn't be able to taste the ice cream very well.

Host: Wow. You do have to be careful with your taste buds.

Peter: Yes, I do. In fact, my taste buds are so important that they are covered by a one million-dollar insurance policy.

Host: One million dollars! You don't say!

Peter: That's right. You see, I have to make sure that all of the ice cream my company makes tastes good. So, if something bad happens to my taste buds and I can't taste the ice cream, my company and I will lose a lot of money. So I need to have a lot of insurance.

Host: Gee, you do have a very important job, Peter. So how did you get started as an ice-cream taster? Did you go to ice-cream tasting school?

Peter: Oh, no. My family has been in the ice-cream business for a long time. My great grandfather owned ice-cream stores, and my grandfather and my father owned ice-cream factories. I've always wanted to work with ice cream, too.

Host: That's great Peter. Thank you very much for being on the show, and keep up the good work! OK everybody, it's time for a commercial break. But, don't go away. We'll be right back with our next guest, on *What's My Job?*

3C. *Listening for Details*

(repeat Section 3B)

3D. *Listening between the Lines*

EXCERPT ONE

Peter: That's right. I work in an ice-cream factory. I taste the ice cream to make sure that it tastes good. I also think of interesting new flavors to make.

Host: Gee, sounds like a difficult job, Peter. You taste ice cream all day and you get paid for it!

Peter: Yes, that's right. I'm lucky to have such a great job. I really love it!

EXCERPT TWO

Host: . . . So how did you get started as an ice-cream taster? Did you go to ice-cream tasting school?

Peter: Oh, no. My family has been in the ice-cream business for a long time. My great grandfather owned ice-cream stores, and my grandfather and my father owned ice-cream factories. I've always wanted to work with ice cream, too.

4. LISTENING TWO: More Offbeat Jobs

4A. *Expanding the Topic*

JOB NUMBER 1

Young man: I'm a window washer. I go high up in the air in a basket to reach the windows on tall office buildings, so I can wash them. I really like my job because I enjoy being outdoors. I like to breathe the fresh air and look at the beautiful views of the city. It's really relaxing. And I earn a high salary. But . . . my job is dangerous. I have to be very careful not to fall out of the basket, and I have to be careful not to drop things on people below. This is a great job for me because I'm good with my hands, and I don't mind doing dangerous work. Even so, it was difficult for me to get started as a window washer. But now, I have my own business. It's great!

JOB NUMBER 2

Middle-aged Woman: I'm a professional shopper. I go shopping for people who are busy and don't have time to shop. People give me a shopping list and some money, and I do the shopping for them. I like my job because I love to shop and I really like to work with people. I'm also very good with money. My job is great, but it isn't that easy. I'm on my feet a lot, so my work is tiring. And it wasn't easy to get started as a shopper. I worked for many years as a salesclerk in a department store. Then I started to meet people who needed a shopper. When I had enough customers, I quit my job at the department store and started my own business.

(repeat Section 4A)

5. REVIEWING LANGUAGE

5A. *Exploring Language*

<u>care</u>ful

pro<u>fess</u>ional

hard<u>work</u>ing

❶ 1. friendly
   2. important
   3. relaxing
   4. educated
   5. creative

UNIT 2 ◆ A PIECE OF THE COUNTRY IN THE CITY

3. LISTENING ONE: Community Gardens

3A. *Introducing the Topic*

Reporter: Hi, I'm Laura Lee from WNYZ News Radio here in New York City. I'm standing in front of a community garden. Community gardens are gardens in cities that many people make together. Each person uses a small area to plant a garden. Together, they make a community garden. It's a nice way to have a little piece of the country in the city or the suburbs.

The city of New York let people in the neighborhood use this empty lot to make a community garden. But now, the city of New York wants to remove the garden. Let's go talk to someone and see what he thinks about it. Hello . . . How are you doing?

3B. *Listening for Main Ideas*

Reporter: Hi, I'm Laura Lee from WNYZ News Radio here in New York City. I'm standing in front of a community garden. Community gardens are gardens in cities that many people make together. Each person uses a small area to plant a garden. Together, they make a community garden. It's a nice way to have a little piece of the country in the city or the suburbs.

The city of New York let people in the neighborhood use this empty lot to make a community garden. But now, the city of New York wants to remove the garden. Let's go talk to someone and see what he thinks about it. Hello . . . How are you doing?

Man: Oh, hello.

Reporter: Hi, I'm from WNYZ News Radio. I understand the city wants to remove this garden. Is that correct?

Man: Yes, that's right. Can you believe it? After all this work we've done.

Reporter: You don't sound happy.

Man: I'm not. You see, ten years ago before we planted the garden, this was just an empty lot. The city gave us this empty lot to make a community garden. All the people in the neighborhood worked really hard. We planted *everything* you see . . . flowers, vegetables, trees. We worked together and made this community garden.

Reporter: The garden does make the neighborhood look nice.

Man: You bet it does. You should have seen this place before we planted the garden. It had garbage on it and people just hung around. We made it beautiful. Now, the city wants to remove all of this to build apartment buildings.

Reporter: Well, we all know there are not enough apartments in New York . . . right?

Man: Yeah, I know that's a problem. But there are other empty lots in the city. They can build apartments there.

Reporter: I see. So the garden is more important than apartments?

Man: Well, I didn't say that. Of course apartments are important. But neighborhoods are important, too. We made this neighborhood a nice place to live.

Reporter: Are there other reasons this garden is important?

Man: Sure. Before we planted the garden, we didn't have a place to enjoy nature. There isn't a lot of nature in the city, you know.

Reporter: Yes, I know what you mean.

Man: This neighborhood didn't have trees or flowers. People had no place to come and sit. You know, get together with their friends and talk or just relax. Children didn't have a place to play either. Now, there is a place for children to play and people to relax or meet their friends. We have a small part of the country in the city now and a place to enjoy nature.

Reporter: Hmm. It sounds like the garden is really good for the people in the neighborhood.

Man: Yeah, it is. Before we planted this garden, some people sold drugs here. They didn't have jobs and didn't know how to do anything. Then they joined this garden and learned how to grow food. Now, they sell vegetables, not drugs.

Reporter: So this garden gave people jobs.

Man: Yeah. And another thing. There are people like me. I grew up in the country. My family grew all our food. When I moved to the city, I lived in an apartment building with no yard so I couldn't grow food anymore. In this community garden, I can grow vegetables again.

Reporter: Yeah, it's true. Most people don't have a place to grow food in the city.

Man: That's right. That's another reason this garden is so important to us.

Reporter: I understand. Well, thank you for telling us about this community garden. I hope the city doesn't build on it.

Man: Yeah. I hope people hear this story on the radio and help us save our garden. Thanks for coming out here.

Reporter: OK. Good luck. . . .

Man: Take care.

Reporter: So, community gardens really give people a small part of the country in the middle of the city. They also make the neighborhood a nicer place to live. Tomorrow night, we will find out what New York plans to do. Will they build apartments and remove this garden . . . or not? Until then, good night.

3C. *Listening for Details*

(repeat Section 3B)

3D. *Listening between the Lines*

EXCERPT ONE

Reporter: The garden does make the neighborhood look nice.

Man: You bet it does. You should have seen this place before we planted the garden. It had garbage on it and people just hung around. We made it beautiful. Now, the city wants to remove all of this to build apartment buildings.

EXCERPT TWO

Man: Yeah. And another thing. There are people like me. I grew up in the country. My family grew all our food. When I moved to the city, I lived in an apartment building with no yard so I couldn't grow food anymore. In this community garden, I can grow vegetables again.

4. LISTENING TWO: Let's Hear from Our Listeners

4A. *Expanding the Topic*

Host: Good afternoon and welcome to *Talk of the Town*. I'm Juana Ramon and we just heard a great story about community gardens in New York. You know, community gardens are one kind of urban greening or urban beautification. They make a city green and beautiful. Today, we want to hear from you, our listeners. What urban greening programs do you see in the city? How do people help make the city beautiful? Let's hear from our first caller. Hello. You're on the air.

Man 1: Yeah, hi. I live in a really nice neighborhood. About five years ago, all the neighbors got together and planted trees. One tree in front of each house. Now, there are beautiful trees all along the street. The trees make the street shady and cool in the summer and they make the neighborhood green.

Host: Great! So the neighbors planted trees in the neighborhood. That's a great way to make a city greener. OK. Let's hear from another caller. You're on the air.

Woman 1: Hi. Well, I live in a tall apartment building. There are no empty lots in my neighborhood and there aren't any trees. But we do have a really nice garden on our roof. We have a roof garden and I really enjoy going there to relax. We have small trees and flowers . . . It's really wonderful.

Host: Roof gardens. What a great idea! There are a lot of apartments and tall buildings in the city. Why not plant a garden on top of a building! Let's hear from one more caller. Good afternoon . . . You're on the air.

Man 2: Hi, yeah. Um, I work for a large company and we decided to help make the city clean and beautiful by picking up garbage along the highway. It's called "Adopt-a-Highway." Our company agrees to take care of one mile of the highway and pick up the garbage. It helps keep the city clean and beautiful.

Host: Yes, I have seen the "Adopt-a-Highway" signs on the side of the road. That's another wonderful way to help keep cities green and beautiful. Well, that's about all the time we have this afternoon. We've heard some great examples of urban greening and beautification. Until next week, this is Juana Ramon for *Talk of the Town* saying good-bye.

5. REVIEWING LANGUAGE

5A. *Exploring Language*

   1. I worked in a community garden yesterday.

2. She planted some vegetables last week.

3. My children played on an empty lot near my home.

4. I walked on a beautiful tree-lined street today.

5. Last week, the city removed the garbage from the empty lot.

6. Everyone liked the flowers in the community garden.

7. My family lived in a city last year.

8. They stayed in the garden late yesterday.

9. I wanted to visit the country last weekend.

10. We watched the children playing.

UNIT 3 ◆ A PENNY SAVED IS A PENNY EARNED

3. LISTENING ONE: Money Problems

3A. *Introducing the Topic*

Advisor: Good morning. I'm Susan Anderson. I'll be your money management advisor.

Henry: Hello. I'm Henry Williams. This is my wife, Carol.

Advisor: Nice to meet you. Please have a seat.

Henry and Carol: Thank you.

Advisor: So, Henry and Carol, I understand you're having some money problems . . .

Henry: Yes, you see we just got married last year and we've been in debt ever since. We have so many bills and we can't pay them all. We need to get out of debt, but we don't know what to do.

Advisor: Don't worry. Many young people have money problems. And you did the right thing by coming to see an advisor. I'll look at how much money you earn and how much money you spend, and I'll help you to make a budget so you can save some money.

3B. *Listening for Main Ideas*

Advisor: Good morning. I'm Susan Anderson. I'll be your money management advisor.

Henry: Hello. I'm Henry Williams. This is my wife, Carol.

Advisor: Nice to meet you. Please have a seat.

Henry and Carol: Thank you.

Advisor: So, Henry and Carol, I understand you're having some money problems . . .

Henry: Yes, you see we just got married last year and we've been in debt ever since. We have so many bills and we can't pay them all. We need to get out of debt, but we don't know what to do.

Advisor: Don't worry. Many young people have money problems. And you did the right thing by coming to see an advisor. I'll look at how much money you earn and how

much money you spend, and I'll help you to make a budget so you can save some money.

Carol: Oh, that's great!

Advisor: Well, it's not going to be easy. To get out of debt you need to spend less money than you earn. Let's begin by looking at your income. How much money do you earn every month?

Henry: We earn $3,000 a month.

Advisor: OK. Now let's look at some of your expenses. How much do you spend on housing?

Henry: We rent an apartment for $1,800 a month.

Advisor: Eighteen hundred dollars? That's a lot of money for an apartment. . . .

Carol: I know . . . But it's such a great apartment. It's big, and it has a beautiful view.

Advisor: It sounds very nice, but beautiful views don't pay the bills. You really need to find a cheaper place to live. Don't spend more than 35 percent of your income on rent.

Henry: I told you our apartment was too expensive!

Carol: Not now Henry! Well, Susan . . . We'll see what we can do.

Advisor: Good. Now let's look at your transportation costs. How do you both get to work?

Carol: I take the bus to work.

Advisor: And how about you, Henry?

Henry: I drive to work.

Advisor: So, you drive a car. Do you have car payments?

Henry: Yes.

Advisor: How much do you pay?

Henry: Five hundred dollars a month . . . I know that's a lot, but it's a new car. It's really nice.

Advisor: I see. Well, I'm sure your car is nice, but it's also very expensive. I think you should sell your car. Buy a used car, or better yet, take the bus to work. The bus is slower and less convenient than driving, but it's also much cheaper.

Henry: Sell my car? But . . . But what will my friends think when they see me driving an old, used car or riding the bus?

Advisor: I think you need to think less about what your friends think, and more about saving money.

Carol: I agree! I never wanted Henry to buy that car. It's a big waste of money!

Advisor: OK. OK. Now I want to look at your credit card debt. How many credit cards do you have?

Henry: Carol's the one to ask about that. She's the one who uses credit cards.

Carol: Well, let me think . . . I think I have twelve, no make that thirteen, credit cards.

Advisor: Thirteen! That's a lot of credit cards. To save money, you really need to stop using your credit cards until you finish paying the bills. Use cash to pay for things instead.

Carol: But using a credit card is so much easier than paying with cash.

Advisor: Well, I agree that using a credit card is easy, but they are also very expensive to use. If you don't pay the credit card company all the money you owe them every month, they will charge you interest. The interest can get very expensive. It's much cheaper to pay with cash.

Carol: I guess you're right . . . But I never have enough cash to pay for everything, like when I go shopping or out to lunch with my friends.

Advisor: Then you need to spend less money and only buy things you really need. By the way, how much *do* you spend every month on shopping and eating out?

Carol: How much? Well, I don't really know . . . But . . . But Henry spends a lot of money too.

Advisor: I'm sure he does. So, I think that *both* of you should write down all of your expenses, so we can find out how much money you do spend. For the next two weeks, I want you to write down everything you buy and how much money you spend.

Carol: Write down *all* of our expenses? For two weeks?

Advisor: Yes, it will help me to find more ways for you to save money.

Henry: OK, we'll give it a try. Thank you for your help.

Carol: Yes, thank you for your advice, Susan.

Advisor: You're welcome. I'll see you in two weeks. And good luck!

3C. *Listening for Details*

(repeat Section 3B)

3D. *Listening between the Lines*

EXCERPT ONE

Henry: We rent an apartment for $1,800 a month.

Advisor: Eighteen hundred dollars? That's a lot of money for an apartment. . . .

Carol: I know . . . But it's such a great apartment. It's big, and it has a beautiful view.

Advisor: It sounds very nice, but beautiful views don't pay the bills. You really need to find a cheaper place to live. Don't spend more than 35 percent of your income on rent.

Henry: I told you our apartment was too expensive!

Carol: Not now Henry! Well, Susan . . . We'll see what we can do.

EXCERPT TWO

Advisor: I see. Well, I'm sure your car is nice, but it's also very expensive. I think you should sell your car. Buy a used car, or better yet, take the bus to work. The bus is slower and less convenient than driving, but it's also much cheaper.

Henry: Sell my car? But . . . But what will my friends think when they see me driving an old car or riding the bus?

Advisor: I think you need to think less about what your friends think, and more about saving money.

Carol: I agree! I never wanted Henry to buy that car. It's a big waste of money!

4. LISTENING TWO: Saving Money

4A. *Expanding the Topic*

❶ CONVERSATION 1

A: What are you doing?

B: I'm clipping these coupons out of the newspaper. Then I'm going to the supermarket.

A: Do you really save money with coupons? It takes so much time . . .

B: Oh, yes, I always clip coupons for the things we need. Last week I saved fifteen dollars on food.

A: Wow, that's great. Maybe I should start using coupons.

CONVERSATION 2

A: Hey, I like your new furniture. Where did you get it?

B: You'll never believe it, but I bought it used at a thrift store.

A: A thrift store, huh?

B: Yeah, and the best part is, it was really cheap. I saved at least two hundred dollars buying my furniture used instead of new.

A: It's great that you saved money, but I would never buy anything used. I only like to buy new things.

CONVERSATION 3

A: Hey, where are you going?

B: I'm going to the outlet center. I want to go shopping for some new clothes.

A: The outlet center? Isn't that far away?

B: Yes, it is pretty far away. It's out in the suburbs.

A: That's not very convenient . . .

B: I know. The outlets are less convenient than the department stores, and sometimes there aren't any salesclerks to help you, but the clothes are a lot less expensive. Last time, I found a jacket for 50 percent off the regular price. I saved seventy-five dollars!

A: Seventy-five dollars! Wow!

B: So, do you want to come with me?

A: OK. Why not! Maybe I'll save some money!

❷ (repeat Section 4A)

5. REVIEWING LANGUAGE

5A. *Exploring Language*

13	30
/thir<u>teen</u>/	/<u>thir</u>dy/

❶ 1. 13   5. 70

    2. 40   6. 18

    3. 50   7. 19

    4. 16

❸ four dollars and twenty-nine cents
four twenty-nine
fifty-three dollars and ninety-nine cents
fifty-three ninety-nine

1. seven dollars and fifty cents
2. eighty-three twenty-five
3. three hundred-nineteen dollars and forty cents
4. sixteen ninety-nine
5. fifteen hundred dollars

UNIT 4 ◆ AT YOUR SERVICE: SERVICE ANIMALS

3. LISTENING ONE: Kimba, the Hero Dog

3A. *Introducing the Topic*

Steve: . . . so we can look forward to sunny skies and warm weather this weekend. Our next story is reported by Ann Lycoff. She is reporting on a fire. Ann.

Ann: Thanks, Steve. I'm here at what was the scene of a fire. This house caught on fire this morning. Firefighters arrived quickly and everyone was safe. But it was a close call. You see, the woman who lives here, Mrs. Ravenscroft, is deaf. When the fire started, the fire alarm went off. Mrs. Ravenscroft couldn't hear the alarm. But thanks to her dog, Kimba, she's OK now.

3B. *Listening for Main Ideas*

Steve: . . . so we can look forward to sunny skies and warm weather this weekend. Our next story is reported by Ann Lycoff. She is at the scene of a fire. Ann.

Ann: Thanks, Steve. I'm here at what was the scene of a fire. This house caught on fire this morning. Firefighters arrived quickly and everyone was safe. But it was a close call. You see, the woman who lives here, Mrs. Ravenscroft, is deaf. When the fire started, the fire alarm went off. Mrs. Ravenscroft couldn't hear the alarm. But thanks to her dog, Kimba, she's OK now.

Steve: So what happened, Ann?

Ann: Well, the fire started in the kitchen. Mrs. Ravenscroft was in the living room and did not hear the alarm. Kimba did hear the alarm and started running up and down the hall from the kitchen to the living room. Mrs. Ravenscroft saw the dog running and knew something was wrong. Mrs. Ravenscroft went to the kitchen and saw the fire. Flames were already three feet high! She immediately called 911 and the fire department came. Without the dog, she would not have known there was an alarm. Kimba saved Mrs. Ravenscroft's life. Mrs. Ravenscroft is very lucky. As you might guess, this is not just any dog. This is a special dog. Kimba is a hearing dog.

Steve: Huh. A hearing dog. What do hearing dogs do, Ann?

Ann: Well, hearing dogs are specially trained to assist deaf people. Hearing dogs tell deaf people about many different sounds, for example, the doorbell ringing, a baby crying, a fire alarm or the telephone ringing, and many more sounds, too. Hearing dogs go to special schools where they are trained how to tell deaf people about important sounds.

Steve: So why do deaf people use hearing dogs?

Ann: Well, think about one of your days and all the sounds you hear: the alarm clock in the morning, the timer on the microwave, a knock on the door, a sound from your computer. All these sounds provide such important information. Now imagine for a minute that you couldn't hear *any* of those sounds. Your life would be very different. We don't think about hearing sounds because we *can* hear them. So the hearing dogs can tell their deaf owners about all these important sounds that we hear all the time, but don't think about.

Steve: How do hearing dogs do it? How do they tell people about sounds?

Ann: Well, when the dog hears a sound, for example the doorbell, the dog first goes to the deaf person. The dog touches the deaf person to get their attention and then the deaf person knows the dog is trying to tell them something. Next, the dog goes to the sound, in this example, the door. The deaf person then knows that someone is ringing the doorbell or knocking on the door.

Steve: Where do deaf people use their hearing dogs?

Ann: Deaf people use hearing dogs in their homes of course, but like I said before, sounds are everywhere—at work, on the bus, or on the street. So, deaf people bring their dogs with them everywhere they go. Also, hearing dogs can go into all public places, such as restaurants and stores. Basically, a hearing dog can go to work, on the bus, and out to dinner, too!

Steve: So, are hearing dogs just service animals?

Ann: Well, hearing dogs are service animals, but hearing dogs are also companions. They are good friends to their owners. Like I said, they can do and go everywhere with their owners.

Steve: Interesting.

Ann: Yes, it really is. So, Mrs. Ravenscroft didn't hear the alarm, but her companion and hearing dog, Kimba, did. Before the fire, Mrs. Ravenscroft called Kimba her personal hearing dog. Now, Mrs. Ravenscroft says Kimba is her personal hero dog because Kimba saved her life! So, tonight our story has a happy ending and everyone is safe! Back to you, Steve.

Steve: That's a very interesting story and good information on hearing dogs, too. Thank you, Ann. And that's the news for this evening. Until tomorrow . . . Good night.

3C. *Listening for Details*

(repeat Section 3B)

3D. *Listening between the Lines*

EXCERPT ONE

Ann: Well, hearing dogs are specially trained to assist deaf people. Hearing dogs tell deaf people about many different sounds, for example, the doorbell ringing, a baby crying, a fire alarm or the telephone ringing, and many more sounds, too. Hearing dogs go to special schools where they are trained how to tell deaf people about important sounds.

EXCERPT TWO

Ann: Deaf people use hearing dogs in their homes of course, but like I said before, sounds are everywhere—at work, on the bus, or on the street. So, deaf people bring their dogs with them everywhere they go. Also, hearing dogs can go into all public places, such as restaurants and stores. Basically, a hearing dog can go to work, on the bus, and out to dinner, too!

4. LISTENING TWO: Do People Help Animals, Too?

4A. *Expanding the Topic*

Man: Good morning, honey.

Woman: Hi, dear.

Man: Anything interesting in the paper today?

Woman: Yes. Listen to this . . . "Bruno, a six-month-old dog, is safe and happy tonight . . ."

Man: Is this another dog story because I really don't want to hear . . .

Woman: No, no, no. Just listen . . . Bruno, a young, curious dog, wandered off from his home last night. It seems he went into a sewer pipe on the street. I guess he went in too far, because he couldn't get out—he got stuck inside. When he didn't come home, his owners walked all over the neighborhood calling his name. Bruno heard his owners calling his name and got their attention by crying. Finally, his owners figured out where he was. They immediately called a company who came out and was able to save the poor dog. So tonight, he's safe at home again with his owners. What a lucky dog, don't you think?

Man: Yeah, yeah. So, a dog got lost and someone saved him.

Woman: It says here that the company usually charges about ten thousand dollars for the work they did. But they were so happy that the dog was safe, they did the work for free! Isn't that great!

Man: Well, that's a good use of money. Ten thousand dollars . . . I could do a lot with ten thousand dollars . . .

Woman: Honey—what about the poor dog? They couldn't just leave him there. He would die . . .

Man: It's a dog!

Woman: Right.

❸ (repeat Section 4A)

5. REVIEWING LANGUAGE

5A. *Exploring Language*

What do service animals do?

What does a hearing dog do?

Where do hearing dogs go?

❶ 1. What do service animals do?

   2. What do hearing dogs do?

   3. Where do deaf people use hearing dogs?

   4. Why do deaf people use hearing dogs?

   5. What do you think about hearing dogs?

UNIT 5 ◆ SURFING IN THE SKY

3. LISTENING ONE: The Competition

3A. *Introducing the Topic*

Announcer: Ten points . . . great! Five points . . . next team . . .

Anna: Hi, I'm Anna Lee.

Jerry: And I'm Jerry Daniels, and we are here watching an exciting new sports competition.

Anna: Maybe you've seen surfers at the beach. Surfers stand on a surfboard and ride on the waves in the ocean.

Jerry: And maybe you know about skydiving. In skydiving, the sky diver jumps from an airplane with a parachute on his or her back. The parachute opens and the sky diver falls slowly to the ground.

Anna: But do you know about surfers who jump from airplanes? They're called sky surfers.

Jerry: And today, we're watching a sky-surfing competition.

3B. *Listening for Main Ideas*

Anna: Hi, I'm Anna Lee.

Jerry: And I'm Jerry Daniels, and we are here watching an exciting new sports competition.

Anna: Maybe you've seen surfers at the beach. Surfers stand on a surfboard and ride on the waves in the ocean.

Jerry: And maybe you know about skydiving. In skydiving, the sky diver jumps from an airplane with a parachute on his or her back. The parachute opens and the sky diver falls slowly to the ground.

Anna: But do you know about surfers who jump from airplanes? They're called sky surfers.

Jerry: And today, we're watching a sky-surfing competition.

Anna: Sky surfing is a team sport. There are two people on a team: a sky surfer and a video camera operator. The video camera operator videotapes the sky surfer in the air while the sky surfer does gymnastics. After they've landed, the judges watch the videotape. The team gets points for good gymnastics in the air and good sky surfing.

Jerry: Well then, let's go and see what's happening. We're watching the first team—Michelle and Mike. They're standing next to the airplane. Michelle is wearing special sky-surfing clothes and a helmet on her head. She's holding her sky board.

Anna: And those boards aren't cheap!

Jerry: No, they aren't. A sky board costs more than six hundred dollars! And Michelle's partner is Mike. Mike is going in the airplane, too. He isn't holding a sky board. He's holding a video camera. He's wearing a special helmet, too. He's putting the video camera *on* his helmet so he's wearing the video camera on his head. They're both wearing back-packs. Inside the backpacks are parachutes. All right . . . They look ready. Now they're getting in the airplane and . . . There goes the airplane.

Anna: The plane is going to 15,000 feet. Isn't that correct, Jerry?

Jerry: Yes, Anna. That's correct.

Anna: And OK . . . The plane is now flying at 15,000 feet.

Jerry: Great. The team is getting ready to sky surf. I see the door opening and I see Michelle and Mike standing in the door. They're looking down . . . They're getting ready to jump and . . . There they go. Now they're falling. They are falling *really* fast!

Anna: Yes, that's right, Jerry. Sky surfers fall 120 miles per hour.

Jerry: One hundred twenty miles per hour?

Anna: Yes. They fall 120 miles per hour for one minute without a parachute!

Jerry: That sounds dangerous!

Anna: Well, that's half the fun! Look at that! Michelle is sky surfing! She's standing *on* the sky board and doing gymnastics in the air. She's falling and flipping in the air. Mike is falling with her. He isn't doing gymnastics though. He's videotaping everything.

Jerry: Oh, my . . . They're falling really fast now. When is that parachute going to open?

Anna: OK, now they're at 5,000 feet . . . and . . . there it is. The parachute is opening.

Jerry: That was a long minute! Whew! I feel *much* better now. . . .

Anna: OK. She's getting closer to the ground . . . closer . . . closer . . . and . . . they're on the ground now. Wow! That was exciting! Mike is taking the videotape out of the camera and giving it to the judges. Michelle and Mike both look very happy.

Jerry: Yes, they do. I'm happy, too, now that they're stand-ing on the ground and not falling through the air.

Anna: Now the judges are watching the tape and everyone is waiting.

Jerry: What a sport. Falling 120 miles per hour from 15,000 feet! Doing gymnastics in the air. I'm exhausted just watching!

Anna: Hey, Jerry. Want to try some sky surfing?

Jerry: No, thanks. I like watching sky surfing from the ground! Anna . . . Anna where are you going?

Anna: I'm going sky surfing!

3C. *Listening for Details*

(repeat Section 3B)

3D. *Listening between the Lines*

EXCERPT ONE

Jerry: Great. The team is getting ready to sky surf. I see the door opening and I see Michelle and Mike standing in the door. They're looking down . . . They're getting ready to jump and . . . There they go. Now they're falling. They are falling *really* fast!

EXCERPT TWO

Anna: Yes, that's right, Jerry. Sky surfers fall 120 miles per hour.

Jerry: One hundred twenty miles per hour?

Anna: Yes. They fall 120 miles per hour for one minute without a parachute!

Jerry: That sounds dangerous!

EXCERPT THREE

Jerry: Oh, my . . . They're falling really fast now. When is that parachute going to open?

EXCERPT FOUR

Jerry: That was a long minute! Whew! I feel *much* better now.

4. LISTENING TWO: Other Sports

4A. *Expanding the Topic*

Annabelle: Hi, I'm Annabelle. I really like to be outside. I like to breathe fresh air. I also like to fly. I like to see the view from high in the sky. I like the smell and the feel of fresh air.

Louis: Hi, I'm Louis. What do I like? Well, winter's my favorite time of year. I like to be outdoors and in the snow. I really like the mountains. I also love going fast . . . I enjoy danger!

Susan: I'm Susan. I'm not afraid of anything! I like to do crazy and dangerous things. I love danger . . . It's exciting. I love to be high on top of mountains and buildings. I get a good feeling when I look down and see people far below me . . . really small. That's exciting!

Mark: Hi, I'm Mark. The ocean is my favorite place. It's so beautiful. I love the water and I really like to swim. I also enjoy the sun. I really like to feel the warmth of the sun on my skin.

5. REVIEWING LANGUAGE

5A. *Exploring Language*

1. I'm falling fast.
2. She isn't jumping.
3. They aren't sky surfing.
4. I'm watching a sports competition.
5. He's doing gymnastics.

UNIT 6 ◆ IS IT WOMEN'S WORK?

3. LISTENING ONE: Who's Taking Care of the Children?

3A. *Introducing the Topic*

Host: Good afternoon and welcome to *The Julie Jones Show.* Today the topic is child care. Most people with young children work and need to use child care. In some families, a relative can take care of the children. But, in the United States, more than 50 percent of all families *pay* for child care—they hire someone to take care of the children. Some people take their children to a day-care center. Some people hire a sitter to take care of the children. And some families hire a nanny. A nanny usually lives with a family and takes care of the children in the family's home every day. Today, we have an unusual nanny to tell us about the job. Let's welcome our nanny . . .

3B. *Listening for Main Ideas*

Host: Good afternoon and welcome to *The Julie Jones Show.* Today the topic is child care. Most people with young children work and need to use child care. In some families, a relative can take care of the children. But, in the United States, more than 50 percent of all families *pay* for child care—they hire someone to take care of the children. Some people take their children to a day-care center. Some people hire a sitter to take care of the children. And some families hire a nanny. A nanny usually lives with a family and takes care of the children in the family's home every day. Today, we have an unusual nanny to tell us about the job. Let's welcome our nanny . . .

Man: Hello.

Host: Well hello, good afternoon, and welcome to the show. You are an *unusual* nanny, aren't you?

Man: Yes, I am. A nanny is usually a woman. But a man can be a nanny, too. A man is a male nanny . . . or a manny. M for man. M-a-n-n-y.

Host: Hmm . . . So you are a manny. Right?

Man: Yes. I'm a manny.

Host: What does a male nanny do?

Man: Well, first of all, a nanny, male or female, is the same thing. It's just one is a man and one is a woman. We do the same thing. A nanny takes care of children. A nanny usually lives with a family, but not always.

Host: And what is a typical day for you?

Man: Well, I usually help the children get ready for school. I help them get dressed, make breakfast and lunch. Sometimes, I take them to school and I always pick them up after school. I usually help with their homework, and we often play together and things like that.

Host: Why do families hire a nanny? Why not hire a sitter?

Man: A sitter and a nanny are different. For one thing, a sitter *never* lives with the family. Also, a sitter usually doesn't do household chores. A nanny, on the other hand, takes care of the children in the child's home every day. The nanny also usually does some household chores. A nanny usually lives with the family, but not always. It's a different kind of child care.

Host: A nanny is not a typical job for a man. I mean, it's a little unusual for a man to take care of children and do household chores, isn't it?

Man: Yeah, some people just don't think men can take care of children. They think child care is a woman's job. I disagree. I like it. I also like doing household chores. A nanny is a good job for me. I don't think it's women's work at all.

Host: And how did you know what a nanny does? I mean how did you learn to be a nanny?

Man: Well, I went to a special school that trains nannies. I studied about children and child care in my classes. There are schools where people can go to learn how to be a nanny.

Host: I see. You went to school and got some training.

Man: Yes, I did.

Host: Do most parents like male nannies?

Man: Some parents do. If someone has a boy, the boy might like a male nanny. A male nanny is like a friend to him.

Host: How exactly did you decide to become a nanny?

Man: Well, I've always really liked children. I decided to go to school to become a nanny because it seemed like a great job! After I went to school, I needed a job and I saw an advertisement for a child-care worker that a woman had put up. It was just the kind of job I wanted, so I applied!

Host: Was she surprised?

Man: Yes, she was very surprised. I was the only man who applied for the job. But she liked me and so she hired me to take care of her children.

Host: So a mother hired you as a nanny. What did her husband think?

Man: At first, her husband didn't like the idea. He thought only women could take care of children.

Host: So what happened?

Man: Well, her husband and I got to know each other and he saw the children really liked me. He saw I was a good child-care worker and that is, after all, what's important.

Host: Well, that's good . . . But I'm trying to imagine how a man might feel about another man living in his house. How did he feel about that?

Man: At first, he didn't like it. You know . . . Sometimes he worked late and I was home . . . alone . . . with his wife.

I think a lot of men might worry . . . But it's my job. That's what I do. After a while, he knew it was OK.

Host: So, are you a father to these children?

Man: No, no, no . . . I am *not* their father. They have a father. He comes home at night. I am a male nanny. I take care of the children when the parents work. It's my job.

Host: Do you have other friends who are male nannies?

Man: Well, now I do. My other friends used to make fun of me. They thought it was strange . . . you know . . . I was doing a woman's job. But they didn't have a job and I did. I thought *that* was pretty funny!

Host: Well, I learned something today. The new child-care workers . . . male nannies. Thank you very much for coming and until next week . . . This is Julie Jones saying good-bye.

3C. *Listening for Details*

(repeat Section 3B)

3D. *Listening between the Lines*

EXCERPT ONE

Host: Do most parents like male nannies?

Man: Some parents do. For example, if someone has a boy, the boy might like a male nanny. A male nanny is like a friend to him.

EXCERPT TWO

Host: So, are you a father to these children?

Man: No, no, no . . . I am *not* their father. They have a father. He comes home at night. I am a male nanny. I take care of the children when the parents work. It's my job.

4. LISTENING TWO: Who Is Right for the Job?

4A. *Expanding the Topic*

CONVERSATION 1

Woman: So Joe. I heard your sister decided to go into the army. What do you think about that?

Man: Well, I don't know. Most of the people in the army are men. I don't think women should be in the army. It's really a man's job. You have to be strong.

Woman: Strong, huh. Don't you think women can be strong?

Man: No, not like a man.

Woman: Oh, I see.

CONVERSATION 2

Man: My daughter just started school. She's six years old. Anyway, I met her new teacher.

Woman: Huh. That's great. Did you like her?

Man: Oh, yes. I liked *him* a lot.

Woman: Oh, *he*. Sorry.

Man: Oh, that's OK. When I went to school, all the teachers were women. It was a woman's job. That was pretty typical.

Woman: Yeah, me too.

Man: I think it's great now that a lot of men teach children. Men and women can both teach children.

Woman: Yeah. There's no difference to me!

Man: Children should see both men and women at school. Boys and girls need to know they can both be teachers when they grow up.

CONVERSATION 3

Woman: My car needs to be fixed. It's making a lot of noise. It's pretty old.

Man: I have a good mechanic.

Woman: Can I have his name?

Man: Uh . . . You can have *her* name.

Woman: Her . . . It's a woman?

Man: Yeah, do you have a problem with that?

Woman: Uh . . . No . . . Not at all. Does she know how to fix cars? Does she have training?

Man: Of course!

Woman: Great! If she knows how to fix cars, that's all I need!

5. REVIEWING LANGUAGE

5A. *Exploring Language*

❶ **Woman:** I've lived in this city for twenty-five years.
Man: Really?

❷ 1. **Woman:** I want to go to an all-women's college.
Man: Really.
Woman: Yeah, I think I'd like it.

2. **Man:** You know, I run thirty miles every day.
Woman: Really.
Man: Really . . . I do!

3. **Woman:** I need some help.
Man: OK.
Woman: Well . . . I need you to . . .

4. **Man:** I want to ask you something.
Woman: Well . . .

5. **Woman:** Could you come over here?
Man: Hmm . . .
Woman: I said, could you come over here please.

6. **Woman:** Do you want to go to the city or to the country?
Man: Hmm . . .

UNIT 7 ◆ GOOD-MOOD FOODS

3. LISTENING ONE: Would You Like to Be on the Radio?

3A. *Introducing the Topic*

(Street sounds)
Larry (slurping soup): Mmm, it smells delicious. What's in it?
Dan (eating cookies): Well, thanks. I hope it works. I'll try anything.
Larry: Who? Me? On the radio? No, thanks.

Jenny: Oh, I was awake all night studying. Now I can't keep my eyes open.

Dan: Oh, my girlfriend just left me, and now I'm all alone.

Barbara: Are you kidding?! I'm in a big hurry. I don't have time for this!

3B. *Listening for Main Ideas*

Host: Good afternoon and welcome to *Street Talk,* the radio show where we talk to people on the street. I'm your host, Marty Moore, the *Street Talk* guy. Today I'm here on Market Street talking to people about food. Everyone knows that some foods taste good and some taste bad. And we also know that some food is good for you and some food is bad for you. But, did you know that eating some foods can change your moods? That's right! Some doctors say that if you're in a bad mood, you can eat a certain food and the food will make you feel better. So let's talk to some people and see what they think about food and moods. Here's someone now. Hi. I'm Marty Moore, the *Street Talk* guy. What's your name?

Larry: Me? My name's Larry. Why . . .

Host: Nice to meet you, Larry. Would you like be on the radio?

Larry: Who? Me? On the radio? No, thanks. I'm a little nervous about being on the radio.

Host: Oh, don't be nervous. Here, have some of this soup. It will help you relax.

Larry: Soup? Mmm, it smells delicious. What's in it?

Host: It's made with chili peppers.

Larry: Wow! That's hot!

Host: Oh, don't worry. Soon you'll feel better. You see, chili peppers have something in them that makes your mouth feel very hot right after you eat them. But they will also help you to relax. The more chili peppers you eat, the more relaxed you will feel.

Larry: I sure hope you're right!

Host: OK, on to the next person. Hi, I'm Marty Moore, the *Street Talk* guy. What's your name?

Jenny: My name's Jenny . . .

Host: Hey Jenny, you look tired. What's the matter?

Jenny: Oh, I was awake all night studying. Now I can't keep my eyes open. I'm just exhausted!

Host: Oh, that's too bad. Here, I have just the thing for you.

Jenny: What's this?

Host: It's your lunch—a hamburger and a banana muffin.

Jenny: But I said I'm *exhausted,* not *hungry.*

Host: I know that. You see, the beef in the hamburger can help you feel more energetic. Beef has a lot of iron. Iron is a mineral that can help you feel more energetic, so you won't feel so tired. And the bananas in the muffin can help you feel better, too. Bananas will also help you to feel more energetic.

Jenny: OK, OK, I'll give it a try.

Host: Let's talk to someone else. Excuse me, I'm Marty Moore, the *Street Talk* guy. What's your name?

Dan: I'm Dan.

Host: Gosh Dan, you look *really* unhappy. What's wrong?

Dan: Oh, my girlfriend just left me, and now I'm all alone. I feel miserable!

Host: Gee, I'm sorry to hear that. Maybe I can help you feel better. Here. Eat some of these chocolate chip cookies. You see, chocolate has something in it that makes you feel more upbeat. Some people even say chocolate can make you feel like you're in love!

Dan: In love? Really?

Host: Yes, and cookies are also made with wheat flour. Wheat can help you to relax and feel more upbeat, too.

Dan: Well, thanks. I hope it works. I'll try anything.

Host: Good luck. OK, let's talk to someone else . . . Hello. What's your name?

Barbara: My name? I'm Barbara. Who wants to know anyway?

Host: Well, I'm Marty Moore, the *Street Talk* guy. Would you like to be on the radio?

Barbara: Are you kidding?! I'm in a big hurry. I don't have time for this!

Host: Wow! You're in a really bad mood. What's the matter?

Barbara: Sorry, but I'm really stressed! I'm late for work, and I'm still waiting for the bus! I hope it gets here soon. I have a lot of work to do, and my boss is going to be angry!

Host: Wow, you really are stressed. Here, I've got just what you need. Eat this turkey sandwich, and drink this glass of orange juice.

Barbara: A turkey sandwich and orange juice? Are you crazy? I need a bus, not food!

Host: Hey, don't be so irritable. I'm just trying to help. You see, turkey can help you to feel more energetic so you can do all of your work and feel less stressed. And the vitamin C in your orange juice can also help you to be in a better mood. It can help you to feel more energetic and it can even help you to feel more upbeat so you won't be so irritable.

Barbara: Thanks anyway, but I don't have time for food. I have to get to work!

Host: Well, our time's up for today. This is Marty, the *Street Talk* guy, saying good-bye for now. And don't forget—eat the right foods, and stay in a good mood.

3C. *Listening for Details*

(repeat Section 3B)

3D. *Listening between the Lines*

EXCERPT ONE

Larry: Soup? Mmm, it smells delicious. What's in it?

Host: It's made with chili peppers.

Larry: Wow! That's hot!

Host: Oh, don't worry. Soon you'll feel better. You see, chili peppers have something in them that makes your mouth feel very hot right after you eat them. But they will also help you to relax. The more chili peppers you eat, the more relaxed you will feel.

Larry: I sure hope you're right!

EXCERPT TWO

Barbara: Sorry, but I'm really stressed! I'm late for work, and I'm still waiting for the bus! I hope it gets here soon. I have a lot of work to do, and my boss is going to be angry!

Host: Wow, you really are stressed. Here, I've got just what you need. Eat this turkey sandwich, and drink this glass of orange juice.

Barbara: A turkey sandwich and orange juice? Are you crazy? I need a bus, not food!

4. LISTENING TWO: What's the Matter?

4A. *Expanding the Topic*

Person 1: I can't believe my boyfriend! He forgot my birthday again. Now I'm sitting at home all alone with nothing to do on my birthday! I don't know how he can do this to me. I just don't think he understands how miserable I feel when he forgets things like this.

Person 2: Boy am I beat! I just started a new job. I really like it, but I have to work long hours. I leave the house every day at 6:30 in the morning, and sometimes I don't get home until 9:00 at night! Then when I get home, I'm just too exhausted to do anything.

Person 3: Oh, no! I have a big test tomorrow, and I don't know what to do. I'm really nervous about it. What if I don't study enough? What if I don't do well? I just know I'm going to make a lot of mistakes!

5. REVIEWING LANGUAGE

5A. *Exploring Language*

❶ s = /s/   s = /z/   s = /ɪz/

s = /s/	s = /z/	s = /ɪz/
carrots	bananas	oranges

❷

apples	chips	hamburgers
chili peppers	dishes	sandwiches
	fats	sweets

UNIT 8 ◆ AN ICE PLACE TO STAY

3. LISTENING ONE: An Unusual Vacation

3A. *Introducing the Topic*

Thank you for calling the Swedish travel telephone hotline. This telephone recording offers all the travel information you need to plan a trip to Sweden. We have information about weather, transportation, lodging, and tourist activities in Sweden. To hear more information about the weather in Sweden, press one. To learn more about transportation to Sweden, press two. For lodging, press three and for tourist activities, press four.

You have pressed three for information about lodging in Sweden. We have information about many kinds of lodging in Sweden. To hear more information about campsites, press one. For information on youth hostels, press two. For information on small inns, press three. To hear about large hotels in Sweden, press four, and for information about a special winter hotel in Sweden, press five.

You have pressed five for a special winter hotel in Sweden.

3B. *Listening for Main Ideas*

Thank you for calling the Swedish travel telephone hotline. This telephone recording offers all the travel information you need to plan a trip to Sweden. We have information about weather, transportation, lodging, and tourist activities in Sweden. To hear more information about the weather in Sweden, press one. To learn more about transportation to Sweden, press two. For lodging, press three and for tourist activities, press four.

You have pressed three for information about lodging in Sweden. We have information about many kinds of lodging in Sweden. To hear more information about campsites, press one. For information on youth hostels, press two. For information on small inns, press three. To hear about large hotels in Sweden, press four, and for information about a special winter hotel in Sweden, press five.

You have pressed five for a special winter hotel in Sweden. Probably the most interesting hotel in Sweden is called the Ice Hotel. This hotel is open only during the winter. It is located in a small town in Swedish Lapland. It's about 125 miles inside the Arctic Circle, so the weather is very cold there in the winter. It sometimes reaches 40 degrees below freezing. In the winter, the days are also very short. On winter days there are sometimes only three hours of sunlight.

Most people visit Sweden in the summer when the weather is warm and the days are long. But adventurous travelers who are looking for an unusual vacation come to Sweden in the winter to stay at the Ice Hotel. You see, the Ice Hotel is open only during the winter because it's made from ice and snow! Every November, when the weather is cold, the hotel is built with several rooms, all made from ice and snow. Then in the spring, when the weather gets warm, the hotel turns into water until the following winter. From December to April guests can stay at the Ice Hotel, but it isn't cheap. A room costs about two hundred dollars a night.

In the Ice Hotel, there are several different kinds of rooms. There are enough guest rooms for forty visitors to sleep there each night, and there are also some other rooms to visit. If you would like a drink, you can visit the bar. Try some of the Swedish vodka. A few drinks will be sure to warm you up! After visiting the bar, you can look at some paintings in the art gallery. The Ice Hotel also has a small church, and some guests even come to get married there! The guest rooms all have tall beds made of snow, but there are no doors on the rooms. There are also no bathrooms. If you need to use the bathroom, you must go to the nearby inn. There aren't any closets for your clothes either. Remember, the Ice Hotel is made of ice and snow, so the rooms are always very cold.

But don't worry about the cold. To stay warm at night, you will sleep in a very warm sleeping bag. And if you still feel cold, you can cover your sleeping bag with reindeer furs. And don't forget to wear your hat to keep your ears warm!

In the morning, there are a few ways to warm up. First, you can go to the nearby inn and take a hot sauna. You can even eat a hot breakfast while you're in the sauna. It will feel great after a cold night in the hotel!

After breakfast, there are many things you can see and do near the Ice Hotel. If you enjoy outdoor winter activities you can go cross-country skiing or snowshoeing. The exercise will warm you up quickly! If you would like to try some other interesting outdoor activities, try dogsledding or snowmobiling. You can enjoy the ride and the beautiful arctic scenery. If you are interested in something more relaxing, you can go ice fishing on the frozen lake. Maybe you'll catch some fish for your dinner!

There are also some indoor activities you can enjoy near the Ice Hotel. First, you can visit a beautiful old wooden church that was built in 1609. Then you can go into a nearby restaurant to warm up and try some of the local Swedish food.

We hope you come to Sweden and visit the Ice Hotel. If you are looking for an unusual trip, we think you'll agree that the Ice Hotel is a nice place to stay. But you must come soon. When winter is over and the weather gets warm, the world's only ice hotel will turn into water until the next winter comes!

3C. *Listening for Details*

(repeat Section 3B)

3D. *Listening between the Lines*

EXCERPT ONE

Probably the most interesting hotel in Sweden is called the Ice Hotel. This hotel is open only during the winter. It is located in a small town in Swedish Lapland. It's about 125 miles inside the Arctic Circle, so the weather is very cold there in the winter. It sometimes reaches 40 degrees below freezing. In the winter, the days are also very short. On winter days there are sometimes only three hours of sunlight.

Most people visit Sweden in the summer when the weather is warm and the days are long. But adventurous travelers who are looking for an unusual vacation come to Sweden in the winter to stay at the Ice Hotel.

EXCERPT TWO

The Ice Hotel also has a small church, and some guests even come to get married there! The guest rooms all have tall beds made of snow, but there are no doors on the rooms. There are also no bathrooms. If you need to use the bathroom, you must go to the nearby inn. There aren't any closets for your clothes either. Remember, the Ice Hotel is made of ice and snow, so the rooms are always very cold. But don't worry about the cold. To stay warm at night, you will sleep in a very warm sleeping bag. And if you still feel cold, you can cover your sleeping bag with reindeer furs. And don't forget to wear your hat to keep your ears warm!

4. LISTENING TWO: Vacations around the World

4A. *Expanding the Topic*

VACATION NUMBER 1

This travel package takes you to sunny southern California. Visit the world famous Disneyland amusement park and have the time of your life! When you aren't having fun at Disneyland, you can go sightseeing and take a tour of Hollywood. Maybe you'll even see some movie stars! You can also go shopping in Los Angeles or visit the art museums. Price includes four nights lodging at the Disneyland hotel and bus tours of all the sights. Travel anytime!

VACATION NUMBER 2

This tour is for the adventurous traveler who loves the outdoors. Go hiking through the Himalayan Mountains of Nepal, and go swimming in the rivers. Enjoy the beautiful views. On this trip, you will sleep outdoors in a campsite and meet other travelers from all over the world. You must be healthy for this vacation because you will walk 10 miles a day and carry your own sleeping bag and food. The price includes airfare, food, tent and sleeping bag, and a travel guide for your two-week adventure. This tour is offered in the spring or fall only.

VACATION NUMBER 3

On this vacation, you will enjoy the warm weather and meet the friendly people of Bali, Indonesia. While in Bali, you can relax on the beach. You can also learn about Balinese history, language, and culture. You can study art or dance with a local artist or you can learn how to cook Balinese food. On this trip, you will stay with a family in their home. One low price includes food and lodging. Airfare is extra. Travel in August or December.

❸ (repeat Section 4A)

5. REVIEWING LANGUAGE

5A. *Exploring Language*

You can ski near the Ice Hotel.

Can you shop?

No, you can't shop.

❶ 1. You can go ice fishing.
 2. You can't take a sauna.
 3. You can't go shopping.
 4. You can visit an old church.
 5. You can't go in the summer.
 6. You can go to a museum.

❷ (repeat exercise 1)

UNIT 9 ◆ STAYING HEALTHY

3. LISTENING ONE: Thin-Fast

3A. *Introducing the Topic*

Man: So don't wait another minute. You should try Thin-Fast Diet Tea today. To order your Thin-Fast, call 1-800-555-THIN. That's 1-800-555-8446. Call today and get eight weeks of Thin-Fast for only $39.99. Yes, that's only $39.99 for the best weight-loss remedy money can buy. And that's not all. We're so sure that you'll be happy with Thin-Fast that we offer a money-back guarantee. If you are not happy with our product, return it to us to get your money back. Call now and become happy, healthy, and thin!

Radio Announcer: This is WRAL radio. Now back to another forty minutes of continuous music . . .

3B. *Listening for Main Ideas*

Man: Are you overweight? Do you feel fat and unhealthy? Do you love to eat fattening foods? Do you hate to exercise? Then you should try our amazing weight-loss remedy, Thin-Fast Diet Tea. Thin-Fast Diet Tea is a drink that will help you to lose weight fast. And the best part is you don't have to exercise, and you don't have to go on a diet. Here's one of our happy customers to tell you about it herself. Mary Ann, what do you think about Thin-Fast Diet Tea?

Mary Ann: Oh, it's terrific! It changed my life.

Man: Really? How did it change your life?

Mary Ann: Well, three months ago I was overweight and unhealthy. I looked terrible and I felt terrible. I loved to eat fattening foods and I hated exercise. I tried many different diets and weight-loss remedies, but nothing worked. I just couldn't lose weight. I was so unhappy! Then one day I decided to try Thin-Fast Diet Tea. It really worked! With Thin-Fast I lost sixty-five pounds in only three months. Now I'm thin and happy. I feel healthy and energetic, and everyone says I look great!

Man: I agree! You look terrific, Mary Ann. It's true. Thin-Fast really works. So tell us, Mary Ann, how do you use Thin-Fast?

Mary Ann: Oh, it's very easy to use. You just drink one cup of Thin-Fast twice a day, once in the morning and once in the evening. That's all! You don't have to exercise, and you don't have to go on a diet.

Man: Really? That sounds too good to be true. So, how does Thin-Fast work?

Mary Ann: Well, Thin-Fast helps you to lose weight in two different ways. First, it stops you from feeling hungry.

Man: That's amazing.

Mary Ann: That's right. After drinking a cup of Thin-Fast, you don't feel hungry, so you will eat less food and lose weight.

Man: That's great. But with Thin-Fast do you have to stop eating fattening foods?

Mary Ann: Not at all! With Thin-Fast, you never have to go on a diet. You can eat all the fattening foods that you love, and you will still lose weight.

Man: How does that work?

Mary Ann: Well, the second way that Thin-Fast works is that it prevents your body from taking in the calories from foods that make you gain weight. It actually prevents 80 percent of the fat and 90 percent of the sugar you eat from turning into fat on your body. That means you can eat all the food you want, and you won't gain weight . . . even if

you don't exercise! With Thin-Fast I ate chocolate and ice cream every day, I never exercised, and I still lost weight.

Man: That's just amazing, Mary Ann. But is Thin-Fast a healthy way to lose weight?

Mary Ann: Oh, yes. It's a very safe and healthy way to lose weight. It doesn't have any side effects at all. In fact, in China people have safely used the natural ingredients in Thin-Fast to lose weight for two thousand years.

Man: Two thousand years?

Mary Ann: That's right. The all-natural ingredients used in Thin-Fast were first used in China two thousand years ago. Today people still use it to lose weight.

Man: So, what's it made of? What are the ingredients of Thin-Fast?

Mary Ann: It's made from 100 percent natural herbs. There's nothing artificial in Thin-Fast.

Man: That's great, but I know that losing weight can make you feel tired. How do you feel when you drink Thin-Fast? Do you feel tired?

Mary Ann: Oh, no. The natural herbs in Thin-Fast will help you to feel more energetic, so you will never feel tired or hungry. You feel healthy and happy while you lose weight.

Man: And how does Thin-Fast taste? Most diet drinks taste terrible.

Mary Ann: Oh, not Thin-Fast. It tastes great. It comes in two delicious flavors, orange and lemon. So losing weight is as easy as drinking a delicious cup of tea.

Man: That's wonderful, Mary Ann. Now I'm sure you'll agree that Thin-Fast is the fast and easy way to lose weight without dieting or exercising.

Mary Ann: That's right!

Man: So don't wait another minute. You should try Thin-Fast Diet Tea today. To order your Thin-Fast, call 1-800-555-THIN. That's 1-800-555-8446. Call today and get eight weeks of Thin-Fast for only $39.99. Yes, that's only $39.99 for the best weight-loss remedy money can buy. And that's not all. We're so sure that you'll be happy with Thin-Fast that we offer a money-back guarantee. If you are not happy with our product, return it to us to get your money back. Call now and become happy, healthy, and thin!

Radio Announcer: This is WRAL radio. Now back to another forty minutes of continuous music . . .

3C. *Listening for Details*

(repeat Section 3B)

3D. *Listening between the Lines*

EXCERPT ONE

Mary Ann: I tried many different diets and weight-loss remedies, but nothing worked. I just couldn't lose weight. I was so unhappy! Then one day I decided to try Thin-Fast Diet Tea. It really worked! With Thin-Fast I lost sixty-five pounds in only three months. Now I'm thin and happy. I feel healthy and energetic, and everyone says I look great!

Man: I agree! You look terrific, Mary Ann.

EXCERPT TWO

Mary Ann: Well, the second way that Thin-Fast works is that it prevents your body from taking in the calories from foods that make you gain weight. It actually prevents 80 percent of the fat and 90 percent of the sugar you eat from turning into fat on your body. That means you can eat all the food you want, and you won't gain weight . . . even if you don't exercise! With Thin-Fast I ate chocolate and ice cream every day, I never exercised, and I still lost weight.

Man: That's just amazing, Mary Ann.

EXCERPT THREE

Man: But is Thin-Fast a healthy way to lose weight?

Mary Ann: Oh, yes. It's a very safe and healthy way to lose weight. It doesn't have any side effects at all. In fact, in China people have safely used the natural ingredients in Thin-Fast to lose weight for two thousand years.

Man: Two thousand years?

Mary Ann: That's right. The all-natural ingredients used in Thin-Fast were first used in China two thousand years ago. Today people still use it to lose weight.

4. LISTENING TWO: Health Problems and Remedies

4A. *Expanding the Topic*

CONVERSATION 1

Woman: Hi. How are you?

Man: Oh, not too well.

Woman: Really? What's the matter?

Man: Well I have a bad stomachache. I think I ate too many chili peppers for lunch.

Woman: Oh, that's too bad. Maybe you shouldn't eat such spicy foods. Why don't you try some peppermint tea?

Man: Peppermint tea?

Woman: Yes, peppermint tea is a natural herbal remedy for stomachaches. It really works!

Man: Thanks anyway, but I'd rather go to the drugstore and get some medicine.

CONVERSATION 2

Woman: (coughing)

Man: Wow, you sound pretty sick. What's wrong?

Woman: Oh, I have a terrible cold. I keep getting a lot of colds and I don't know why.

Man: I'm sorry to hear that. Maybe you ought to take better care of yourself. I think you shouldn't work so hard.

Woman: I think you're right. I do work a lot. But I can't quit my job. There must be something else I can do.

Man: Maybe you should try eating garlic. Garlic is really good for you. It can prevent you from catching so many colds. It really works for me. I take garlic every day, and I never get sick.

Woman: Garlic? But garlic is so bad for your breath!

Man: Not if you take garlic pills. There are no side effects with garlic pills.

Woman: Well, OK. I'll give it a try.

5. REVIEWING LANGUAGE

5A. *Exploring Language*

I was <u>overweight</u> and <u>unhealthy</u>.
I <u>looked</u> <u>terrible</u> and I <u>felt</u> <u>terrible</u>.
I <u>loved</u> to eat <u>fattening</u> foods and I <u>hated</u> <u>exercise</u>.

❷ 1. With <u>Thin-Fast</u>, I lost <u>sixty-five</u> <u>pounds</u> in only <u>three</u> <u>months</u>.
   2. You just drink <u>one cup</u> of <u>Thin-Fast</u> <u>twice</u> a <u>day</u>.
   3. You <u>don't</u> have to <u>exercise</u>, and you <u>don't</u> have to go on a <u>diet</u>.
   4. It's a very <u>safe</u> and <u>healthy</u> way to <u>lose</u> <u>weight</u>.
   5. It's made from <u>100 percent</u> <u>natural</u> <u>herbs</u>.

UNIT 10 ◆ DO YOU BELIEVE IN IT?

3. LISTENING ONE: An Introduction to Dowsing

3A. *Introducing the Topic*

Woman: Good morning and welcome to this introductory workshop on dowsing. I understand that everyone here is interested in dowsing, right?

And I know you all want to learn how to dowse, but first it's important to understand what dowsing is. So this morning, I'll talk about dowsing including a little about the history of dowsing and about some uses of dowsing. The next workshop you'll take, this afternoon, will teach you *how* to dowse. OK? Please feel free to ask questions at any time. All right, let's get started.

3B. *Listening for Main Ideas*

Woman: Good morning and welcome to this introductory workshop on dowsing. I understand that everyone here is interested in dowsing, right?

And I know you all want to learn how to dowse, but first it's important to understand what dowsing is. So this morning, I'll talk about dowsing including a little about the history of dowsing and about some uses of dowsing. The next workshop you'll take, this afternoon, will teach you *how* to dowse. OK? Please feel free to ask questions at any time. All right, let's get started.

So, dowsing. What is it? The original use of dowsing was to find metal or water underground. That's the oldest use of dowsing, and people all over the world have used dowsing for thousands of years. In fact, the oldest pictures of dowsing were found in Africa. They are more than eight thousand years old.

Man: Excuse me. How old did you say the pictures were?

Woman: More than eight thousand years old. So you can see that dowsing is very old. Now a dowser is a person who uses dowsing. A dowser holds a divining rod that lets the dowser find things underground. A dowser holds the diving rod and walks on the ground. The divining rod lets the dowser feel the metal or water underground. The dowser can't see the metal or water but when the divining rod shakes, or moves down toward the ground, the dowser knows metal or water is underground. Ah yes, you have a question, sir?

Man: Yeah. Did you say the dowser can't see the water . . . but he knows the water is underground? What exactly do you mean by that?

Woman: Well, dowsers believe everything has an energy that people can feel. When you use a divining rod, you can feel the energy and find things. That's how dowsing works.

Man: That's a little hard to believe. And what do scientists say about it?

Woman: Well, you can't explain everything using science. Scientists say dowsing doesn't work. But dowsers use it for many things and believe it does work!

Man: Well, if I need to find water underground, I'll just look at a map, and I'll find all the water I need.

Woman: That is one way to find water, but it's not dowsing. Maybe you're in the wrong workshop, sir . . .

Man: Well, I'm just here with my girlfriend. She believes in all this stuff.

Woman: Hmm. I see. Well, you did mention maps, and that leads me to another use of dowsing: map dowsing. As I said, dowsing was used to find things underground. Nowadays people still dowse to find underground water in the United States and Europe, but people also dowse for many other things. Map dowsing is a method dowsers use to find lost people or things. Map dowsers hold a small stone hanging on a piece of string. This is called a pendulum. They hold the pendulum over a map and ask a question about the location of a lost person or thing. The pendulum will swing over a location on the map. The pendulum will show where the lost person or thing is!

Man: That's impossible! How can that work?

Woman: No one knows exactly *how* it works, but people have used it to find lost things. Perhaps you'd be more comfortable waiting outside while we learn about dowsing, hmm?

Man: No, no, I'll try to be quiet.

Woman: Well, one woman hired a map dowser to find an expensive musical instrument that someone had stolen from her. The dowser held the pendulum over the map and asked, "Where is the instrument?" The pendulum swung over the city where the stolen instrument was. The police found the house and the stolen instrument. Ask this happy woman and she'll tell you that map dowsing really *does* work!

Yes, it is very interesting. Another use for dowsing is to get answers to questions. People dowse to get answers to yes/no questions. You can use dowsing to get answers to important questions about work, your health, money, your family, and your future.

Man: OK, OK . . . *I* have a question. Who will answer *my* question about my future? Who knows the future?

Woman: Well, you can use dowsing to find that answer. Let me explain. You use the pendulum to get answers to questions. Let's do an example . . . Sir, will you please come up here.

Man: Who, me?

Woman: Sure . . . You do seem very interested after all! Come on up!

Man: OK.

Woman: All right. Now what would you like to know? What question do you want answered?

Man: Hmm. Let's see. Will I have a happy future? How's that?

Woman: OK. Good question. OK, now let's use the pendulum to find out. First, you have to ask a yes/no question. Go ahead.

Man: Well, OK. Will I have a happy future?

Woman: Good. Now watch the pendulum. It will swing one way for yes and another way for no. Watch closely . . .

Man: Oh, that's ridiculous. Who knows my future anyway? You can't know the future. You can stop now. I don't believe any of this.

Woman: Well, one thing I *do* know about your future is your girlfriend won't be bringing you to any more workshops on dowsing! But, I hope you do have a happy future! Good luck!

So anyway, that is a very short introduction to dowsing. We're going to break for lunch and after lunch, we'll meet again in room 220 at 1:30. You'll learn how to dowse there. So see you all after lunch!

3C. *Listening for Details*

(repeat Section 3B)

3D. *Listening between the Lines*

EXCERPT ONE

Woman: . . . people all over the world have used dowsing for thousands of years. In fact, the oldest pictures of dowsing were found in Africa. They are more than eight thousand years old.

Man: Excuse me. How old did you say the pictures were?

Woman: More than eight thousand years old. So you can see that dowsing is very old.

EXCERPT TWO

Man: Well, if I need to find water underground, I'll just look at a map, and I'll find all the water I need.

Woman: That is one way to find water, but it's not dowsing. . . .

EXCERPT THREE

Woman: All right. Now what would you like to know? What question do you want answered?

Man: Hmm. Let's see. Will I have a happy future? How's that?

Woman: OK. Good question. OK, now let's use the pendulum to find out. First, you have to ask a yes/no question. Go ahead.

Man: Well, OK. Will I have a happy future?

Woman: Good. Now watch the pendulum. It will swing one way for yes and another way for no. Watch closely . . .

Man: Oh, that's ridiculous. Who knows my future anyway? You can't know the future. You can stop now. I don't believe any of this.

4. LISTENING TWO: Other Unexplained Phenomena

4A. *Expanding the Topic*

LISTENING 1

Man: I just went to a great workshop . . . It was about fire walking. Fire walking is just what it sounds like . . . walking on fire! In fire walking, a person can learn to walk on hot fire. I walked across hot fire and my feet didn't burn! Imagine that! I can't explain how it works, but I know I did it! Fire walking teaches a person to concentrate . . . you know . . . think about one thing and not think about many other things. You see, if you learn to concentrate, you can do anything. I think the mind is very powerful and strong.

LISTENING 2

Woman: I saw an interesting show on TV last night. It was about psychokinesis. Psychokinesis means people move things with their minds. *Psycho* means "mind" and *kinesis* means "move." So people use their minds to move things. One man used his mind to bend spoons. Imagine that! He bent a spoon with his mind . . . no hands! He never touched the spoon. That's the power of the mind. Psychic ability is pretty amazing. I don't know how people do it, but they do!

5. REVIEWING LANGUAGE

5A. *Exploring Language*

I will = I'll
you will = you'll
he will = he'll
she will = she'll
it will = it'll
we will = we'll
they will = they'll

Man: When will you learn to dowse?
Woman: I'll learn how to dowse this weekend.

Man: Where will we learn?
Woman: We'll learn at a workshop.

Man: What will he find?
Woman: He'll find underground water.

Man: Who will they see?
Woman: They'll see a dowser.

Man: What will she teach?
Woman: She'll teach dowsing.

ANSWER KEY

UNIT 1 ◆
OFFBEAT JOBS

2B. VOCABULARY FOR COMPREHENSION

1. a	3. b	5. a	7. b	9. a
2. b	4. a	6. b	8. a	10. b

3A. INTRODUCING THE TOPIC

1. b	3. b	5. *Answers will vary.*
2. a	4. a	

3B. LISTENING FOR MAIN IDEAS

1. b	3. c	5. c
2. b	4. a	

3C. LISTENING FOR DETAILS

1. T	3. F	5. T	7. T
2. T	4. T	6. F	8. F

4A. EXPANDING THE TOPIC

❷ Picture 1: <u>1</u>
Picture 2: 2

❸ a. ww, ps
b. ww
c. ww
d. ww
e. ps
f. ps
g. ww
h. ps
i. ww, ps
j. ww, ps

5A. EXPLORING LANGUAGE: Syllable Stress

❶ 1. <u>friend</u>ly   2
2. im<u>por</u>tant   3
3. re<u>lax</u>ing   3
4. <u>ed</u>ucated   4
5. cre<u>a</u>tive   3

5B. WORKING WITH WORDS

❶ 1. quit
2. interesting
3. be careful
4. get started
5. salary
6. lucky

❷ 1. interesting
2. get started
3. quit
4. salary
5. be careful
6. lucky

UNIT 2 ◆
A PIECE OF THE COUNTRY IN THE CITY

2B. VOCABULARY FOR COMPREHENSION

1. i	3. j	5. d	7. a	9. c
2. b	4. h	6. e	8. g	10. f

3A. INTRODUCING THE TOPIC

1. b	2. c	3. *Answers will vary.*

3B. LISTENING FOR MAIN IDEAS

Reasons mentioned: 1, 2, 4

3C. LISTENING FOR DETAILS

True statements: 1, 3, 5, 6, 7, 8, 10

4A. EXPANDING THE TOPIC

"After You Listen" column:
1. The people in the neighborhood.
2. Yes—on the roof
3. They are picking up garbage. It helps keep the city clean and beautiful.

5A. EXPLORING LANGUAGE

❶ Rule number:
1
4
3
2

❷
/t/	/ɪd/	/d/
worked	planted	played
walked	wanted	removed
liked		lived
watched		stayed

5B. WORKING WITH WORDS

❶
1. d	3. h	5. e	7. a
2. f	4. g	6. c	8. b

❷ 1. urban greening   5. empty lot
2. get together   6. hang around
3. roof garden   7. grow up
4. relax

6A. GRAMMAR: Simple Past Tense

❷
walked	had
worked	made
grew	looked
lived	was
went	were
wore	arrived
moved	spoke

6B. STYLE: Expressing Agreement

❶
1. too	3. too	5. either	7. either
2. either	4. either	6. too	8. too

UNIT 3 ◆
A PENNY SAVED IS A PENNY EARNED

2B. VOCABULARY FOR COMPREHENSION

1
1. a	4. a	7. a	10. b
2. b	5. b	8. a	11. a
3. a	6. b	9. b	

2
1. advisor
2. rent
3. spend
4. car

3A. INTRODUCING THE TOPIC

1. b
2. c
3. *Answers will vary.*

3B. LISTENING FOR MAIN IDEAS

1. c	3. a	5. a
2. c	4. b	

3C. LISTENING FOR DETAILS

Income: $3,000; Rent: $1,800; Car payments: $500; Buy a <u>used</u> car or take the <u>bus</u>; Number of credit cards: 13; Pay with <u>cash</u>; Write down expenses for <u>two</u> weeks.

4A. EXPANDING THE TOPIC

Picture A: Conversation 3; clothes; $75
Picture B: Conversation 1; food; $15
Picture C: Conversation 2; furniture; $200

5A. EXPLORING LANGUAGE: Numbers and Prices

1
1. 13	3. 50	5. 70	7. 19
2. 40	4. 16	6. 18	

3
1. $7.50
2. $83.25
3. $319.40
4. $16.99
5. $1500.00

5B. WORKING WITH WORDS

1
1. used
2. cheap
3. have enough
4. regular price
5. view
6. convenient
7. pay interest
8. a waste of money

UNIT 4 ◆
AT YOUR SERVICE: SERVICE ANIMALS

2B. VOCABULARY FOR COMPREHENSION

a. 5	c. 8	e. 6	g. 10	i. 9
b. 4	d. 1	f. 7	h. 2	j. 3

3A. INTRODUCING THE TOPIC

1. b	2. a	3. *Answers will vary.*

3B. LISTENING FOR MAIN IDEAS

Questions answered: 1, 3, 5, 6, 7

3C. LISTENING FOR DETAILS

1. F	3. F	5. F	7. F	9. T
2. F	4. T	6. T	8. T	

4A. EXPANDING THE TOPIC

2 "After You Listen" column:
1. in the sewer pipe
2. the owners and people from a company
3. to save the dog

5B. WORKING WITH WORDS

1. service dog
2. caught on fire
3. safe
4. get her attention
5. trained
6. owns
7. companion
8. saved
9. hero

6A. GRAMMAR: Simple Present Tense—Wh- Questions with *Do*

2 Questions and possible answers:
1. Where does the woman work?
   She works in the circus.
2. What does the woman do every day at work?
   She trains a lion.
3. Where does the lion live?
   The lion lives in a cage. The lion lives at the circus.
4. Who does the lion live with?
   The lion lives with other lions.
5. Where do lions usually live?
   Lions usually live in the wild or in nature.
6. What do lions usually do all day?
   They usually sleep.
7. When do lions sleep?
   Lions usually sleep during the day.
8. What do lions eat?
   Lions eat meat.
9. Why do you think people like to watch circus animals?
   (*Answers will vary.*)
10. What do you think about circus animals?
    (*Answers will vary.*)

6B. STYLE: Asking for More Information

2
1. a	3. a	5. a
2. a	4. b	6. b

UNIT 5 ◆
SURFING IN THE SKY

2B. VOCABULARY FOR COMPREHENSION

1. Judges, points
2. team
3. jump, fall, flip, parachute
4. video camera operator
5. Surfers, board

3B. LISTENING FOR MAIN IDEAS

1. F **2.** T **3.** F **4.** T **5.** F

3C. LISTENING FOR DETAILS

1. b	**3.** b	**5.** a	**7.** a
2. a	**4.** b	**6.** b	**8.** a

3D. LISTENING BETWEEN THE LINES

Excerpt One: excited
Excerpt Two: worried
Excerpt Three: worried, excited
Excerpt Four: relieved
Answers will vary in the last column on the right.

4A. EXPANDING THE TOPIC

2 Annabelle—hang gliding
Louis—skiing
Susan—bungee jumping
Mark—surfing

5A. EXPLORING LANGUAGE

1 **1.** A   **4.** A
2. N   **5.** A
3. N

5B. WORKING WITH WORDS

1
Be	Get	Go
outdoors	points	outdoors
brave	ready	downhill
ready		
on a team		
afraid of heights		

Wear	Use
a helmet	a parachute
a parachute	a board

6A. GRAMMAR: Present Progressive

2 Possible statements:

Picture 1:
They are standing on the ground.
They are wearing helmets.
They are wearing backpacks.
They are wearing goggles.
The woman is holding a sky board.
The man isn't holding a sky board.
The man is holding a video camera.
They aren't jumping.

Picture 2:
The plane is flying.
The woman is sky surfing.
The woman is flipping.
The man is wearing a helmet.
The man is video taping the sky surfer.
They are falling.
They aren't standing.

Picture 3:
They are standing on the ground.
They are standing next to the airplane.
He is holding a video camera.
He is taking the video tape out.
She is taking off her helmet.
They are smiling.
They're not sky surfing.

3 Part A
b. Bungee jumping
c. Gymnastics
d. Surfing
e. Skiing

UNIT 6 ◆
IS IT WOMEN'S WORK?

2B. VOCABULARY FOR COMPREHENSION

a. 5	**c.** 8	**e.** 7	**g.** 1
b. 4	**d.** 2	**f.** 6	**h.** 3

3A. INTRODUCING THE TOPIC

1. b   **2.** b   **3.** *Answers will vary.*

3B. LISTENING FOR MAIN IDEAS

Order of issues:
3 - The difference between a nanny and a sitter
1 - Child care in the United States
2 - What a nanny does
5 - What one husband thinks about male nannies
4 - How this man became a nanny

3C. LISTENING FOR DETAILS

1. a	**3.** a	**5.** b	**7.** b	**9.** a
2. b	**4.** b	**6.** a	**8.** a	**10.** a

4A. EXPANDING THE TOPIC

Conversation 1: men
            You have to be strong.
Conversation 2: both
            Children should see both men and women
            at school.
Conversation 3: both
            If she (the mechanic) knows how to fix cars,
            that's all she (the woman speaking) needs.

5A. EXPLORING LANGUAGE: Intonation

2 **1.** a, rising
2. b, falling
3. b, falling
4. a, rising
5. a, rising
6. b, falling

5B. WORKING WITH WORDS

1 **1.** f   **3.** e   **5.** d   **7.** a
2. b   **4.** g   **6.** c

2 1. strange
2. typical
3. have a problem with
4. there's no difference
5. make fun of
6. disagree
7. agree

UNIT 7 ◆
GOOD-MOOD FOODS

2B. VOCABULARY FOR COMPREHENSION

1 1. a   4. a   7. b
2. a   5. a   8. b
3. b   6. a   9. a

3B. LISTENING FOR MAIN IDEAS

1. T   3. F   5. F
2. F   4. T

3C. LISTENING FOR DETAILS

1. nervous:
   chili peppers - relaxed
2. exhausted:
   beef - energetic
   bananas - energetic
3. miserable:
   chocolate - in love
   wheat flour - relaxed, upbeat
4. stressed:
   turkey - energetic
   orange juice - energetic, upbeat

4A. EXPANDING THE TOPIC

1 Person 1: sad or miserable; Her boyfriend forgot her
         birthday.
Person 2: tired or exhausted; He's working long hours.
Person 3: nervous; He has a big test tomorrow.

5A. EXPLORING LANGUAGE

2 s = /s/
carrots; chips; fats; sweets

s = /z/
bananas; apples; chili peppers; hamburgers

s = /ɪz/
oranges; dishes; sandwiches

5B. WORKING WITH WORDS

1 Be: hot, alone, angry, awake, bad, crazy, delicious, good
for you, hungry, in a bad mood, in a good mood, in a
hurry, stressed

Feel: hot, alone, angry, bad, hungry, stressed

Look: hot, angry, awake, bad, crazy, delicious, hungry,
stressed

Made with: beef, chili peppers

Smell: bad, delicious

Taste: hot, bad, delicious

6A. GRAMMAR: Count and Non-count Nouns

3 A: Do we need any flour?
B: Yes, we need some flour.

A: Do we need any bananas?
B: Yes, we need some bananas.

A: Do we need any milk?
B: Yes, we need some milk.

A: Do we need any coffee?
B: No, we don't need any coffee.

A: Do we need any apples?
B: No, we don't need any apples.

A: Do we need any bread?
B: Yes, we need some bread.

A: Do we need any sugar?
B: No, we don't need any sugar.

A: Do we need any carrots?
B: No, we don't need any carrots.

A: Do we need any orange juice?
B: Yes, we need some orange juice.

A: Do we need any soup?
B: No, we don't need any soup.

6B. STYLE: Politely Expressing Wants

1
Waiter/Waitress	Customer
3	6
5	2
1	4

UNIT 8 ◆
AN ICE PLACE TO STAY

2B. VOCABULARY FOR COMPREHENSION

2
6 cross-country skiing
1 sauna
4 dogsledding
3 snowmobiling
5 ice fishing
2 snowshoeing

3 1. lodging
2. sleeping bag
3. sauna
4. bar

3A. INTRODUCING THE TOPIC

1. b
3. c
2. a
4. *Answers will vary.*

3B. LISTENING FOR MAIN IDEAS

1. F   3. F   5. F
2. T   4. F   6. T

3C. LISTENING FOR DETAILS

Things in the Ice Hotel:
1. guest rooms, 2. a bar, 4. an art gallery, 5. a church,
6. beds, 10. sleeping bags

Things near the Ice Hotel:
1. a sauna, 2. cross-country skiing, 3. snowshoeing,
5. dogsledding, 6. snowmobiling, 8. ice fishing,
10. a restaurant

4A. EXPANDING THE TOPIC

2. Brochure A: vacation #2
   Brochure B: vacation #1
   Brochure C: vacation #3

3. Brochure A
   Activities: go hiking, enjoy the views, meet other travelers
   Lodging: outdoors in a campsite
   Time of Year: spring or fall

   Brochure B
   Activities: visit Disneyland, take a tour of Hollywood,
   go sightseeing/shopping, visit art museums
   Lodging: Disneyland hotel
   Time of Year: anytime

   Brochure C
   Activities: relax on the beach, study art or dance, learn
   how to cook Balinese food
   Lodging: stay with a family in their home
   Time of Year: August or December

5A. EXPLORING LANGUAGE: Word Stress with *Can* and *Can't*

❶ 1. affirmative
   2. negative
   3. negative
   4. affirmative
   5. negative
   6. affirmative

❷ 1. You can go ice fishing.
   2. You can't take a sauna.
   3. You can't go shopping.
   4. You can visit an old church.
   5. You can't go in the summer.
   6. You can go to a museum.

❸ 1. T   3. T   5. T
   2. F   4. T   6. F

5B. WORKING WITH WORDS

❶ 1. g   3. i   5. a   7. c   9. j
   2. h   4. b   6. d   8. e   10. f

❷ Indoor Activities:
   stay at youth hostels, take a sauna

   Outdoor Activities:
   go cross-country skiing, go hiking, relax on the beach

   Indoor or Outdoor Activities:
   be adventurous, go to amusement parks, have fun, look at
   the scenery, take a tour

6B. STYLE: Making Polite Requests

❷ Student A:
   1. across the street
   2. about two dollars
   3. about eight dollars
   4. 11 A.M. to 3 P.M.
   5. 10 A.M. to 2 P.M.
   6. about twenty cents

   Student B:
   1. in Hollywood
   2. about $50
   3. 624-7300
   4. 9 A.M. to midnight
   5. $25
   6. 9 A.M. to 7 P.M.

UNIT 9 ◆
STAYING HEALTHY

2B. VOCABULARY FOR COMPREHENSION

1. c   4. b   7. i   10. k
2. g   5. j   8. f   11. h
3. e   6. a   9. d   12. l

3A. INTRODUCING THE TOPIC

1. a   2. b   3. *Answers will vary.*

3B. LISTENING FOR MAIN IDEAS

1. a   2. b   3. b   4. a   5. b

3C. LISTENING FOR DETAILS

1. F   3. T   5. F   7. F   9. T
2. F   4. T   6. F   8. T   10. T

4A. EXPANDING THE TOPIC

Conversation 1: stomachache; peppermint tea; no
Conversation 2: cold; garlic; yes

5A. EXPLORING LANGUAGE: Sentence Stress

❶ *Answers will vary.*
   1. With Thin-Fast I lost sixty-five pounds in only
      three months.
   2. You just drink one cup of Thin-Fast twice a day.
   3. You don't have to exercise, and you don't have to go
      on a diet.
   4. It's a very safe and healthy way to lose weight.
   5. It's made from 100 percent natural herbs.

5B. WORKING WITH WORDS

❶ 1. terrible
   2. herbal
   3. remedies
   4. too good to be true
   5. prevent
   6. product
   7. take care of yourself
   8. terrific
   9. side effect
   10. money-back guarantee

6A. GRAMMAR: Modal Verbs *Should, Ought to,* and *Have to*

❷ 1. should
2. shouldn't
3. should
4. have to
5. ought
6. should
7. don't have to
8. should

UNIT 10 ◆
DO YOU BELIEVE IN IT?

2B. VOCABULARY FOR COMPREHENSION

❶ 1. f   4. e   7. i   10. k
2. g   5. j   8. c   11. b
3. h   6. a   9. d

❸ A pendulum can swing.
A divining rod can shake.

3A. INTRODUCING THE TOPIC

1. a   2. *Answers will vary.*   3. *Answers will vary.*

3B. LISTENING FOR MAIN IDEAS

1. Dowsing is very old.
2. Dowsing can't be explained scientifically.
3. Map dowsing is a way to find things.
4. People use dowsing to ask about important questions.
5. The man in the audience doesn't believe in dowsing.

3C. LISTENING FOR DETAILS

1. b   3. a   5. c   7. a
2. c   4. b   6. b   8. c

4A. EXPANDING THE TOPIC

Listening 1
Main idea: 3
Details: 1, 3, 4

Listening 2
Main idea: 2
Details: 3

5B. WORKING WITH WORDS

❶ 1. h   3. f   5. e   7. a   9. g
2. d   4. b   6. c   8. i

❷ 1. psychic ability
2. unexplained phenomenon
3. powerful
4. scientific
5. Fire walking
6. That's ridiculous
7. concentration
8. method
9. mind

6A. GRAMMAR: Future with *Will*

❷ Possible questions:

What will I learn in the astrology / palm reading / fire walking workshop?

Who will teach the astrology / palm reading / fire walking workshop?

Where will the astrology / palm reading / fire walking workshop be?

Where will I stay for the astrology / palm reading / fire walking workshop?

How much will the hotel cost for the astrology / palm reading / fire walking workshop?

How much will the astrology / palm reading / fire walking workshop cost?

When will the astrology / palm reading / fire walking workshop be?

Will I learn about _____ in the astrology / palm reading / fire walking workshop?